KU-775-766

WHAT IS HISTORY?

By the same author

A HISTORY OF SOVIET RUSSIA
*in fourteen volumes*

1. THE BOLSHEVIK REVOLUTION, *Volume One*
2. THE BOLSHEVIK REVOLUTION, *Volume Two*
3. THE BOLSHEVIK REVOLUTION, *Volume Three*
4. THE INTERREGNUM
5. SOCIALISM IN ONE COUNTRY, *Volume One*
6. SOCIALISM IN ONE COUNTRY, *Volume Two*
7. SOCIALISM IN ONE COUNTRY, *Volume Three, Part I*
8. SOCIALISM IN ONE COUNTRY, *Volume Three, Part II*
9. *FOUNDATIONS OF A PLANNED ECONOMY, *Volume One, Part I*
10. *FOUNDATIONS OF A PLANNED ECONOMY, *Volume One, Part II*
11. FOUNDATIONS OF A PLANNED ECONOMY, *Volume Two*
12. FOUNDATIONS OF A PLANNED ECONOMY, *Volume Three, Part I*
13. FOUNDATIONS OF A PLANNED ECONOMY, *Volume Three, Part II*
14. FOUNDATIONS OF A PLANNED ECONOMY, *Volume Three, Part III*

MICHAEL BAKUNIN
INTERNATIONAL RELATIONS BETWEEN THE TWO WORLD WARS, 1919–1939
THE TWENTY YEARS' CRISIS, 1919–1939
NATIONALISM AND AFTER
THE NEW SOCIETY
1917: BEFORE AND AFTER
FROM NAPOLEON TO STALIN
THE RUSSIAN REVOLUTION FROM LENIN TO STALIN, 1917–1929
THE TWILIGHT OF COMINTERN, 1930–1935
THE COMINTERN AND THE SPANISH CIVIL WAR

* *with R. W. Davies*

NEWMAN UNIVERSITY COLLEGE LIBRARY

WITHDRAWN

N 0131939 6

# WHAT IS HISTORY?

by
E. H. CARR

with a new introduction by
Richard J. Evans

NEWMAN UNIVERSITY
COLLEGE
BARTLEY GREEN
BIRMINGHAM B32 3NT

CLASS 901

BARCODE 01319396

AUTHOR CAR

palgrave

© E. H. Carr 1961
© Estate of E. H. Carr 1986
Editorial matter and selection for the second edition © R. W. Davies 1986
Introduction to this edition © R. J. Evans 2001

All rights reserved. No reproduction, copy or transmission of
this publication may be made without written permission.

No paragraph of this publication may be reproduced, copied or
transmitted save with written permission or in accordance with
the provisions of the Copyright, Designs and Patents Act 1988,
or under the terms of any licence permitting limited copying
issued by the Copyright Licensing Agency, 90 Tottenham Court
Road, London W1T 4LP.

Any person who does any unauthorised act in relation to this
publication may be liable to criminal prosecution and civil
claims for damages.

The author has asserted his right to be identified
as the author of this work in accordance with the
Copyright, Designs and Patents Act 1988.

First edition 1961
Reprinted 1961, 1962 (twice), 1969, 1972, 1977, 1982
Second edition 1986
Reprinted with new Introduction 2001

Published by
PALGRAVE
Houndmills, Basingstoke, Hampshire RG21 6XS and
Companies and representatives throughout the world

PALGRAVE is the new global academic imprint of
St. Martin's Press LLC Scholarly and Reference Division and
Palgrave Publishers Ltd (formerly Macmillan Press Ltd).

ISBN 0–333–97701–7 hardback

This book is printed on paper suitable for recycling and
made from fully managed and sustained forest sources.

A catalogue record for this book is available
from the British Library.

10
10 09 08 07 06

Printed and bound in Great Britain by
Antony Rowe Ltd, Chippenham, Wiltshire

'I often think it odd that it should be so dull,
for a great deal of it must be invention.'

CATHERINE MORLAND on History
(*Northanger Abbey*, ch. xiv)

# Contents

# Introduction

## Richard J. Evans

### I

E. H. CARR (1892–1982) was not a professional historian in any sense of the term that would be acceptable today. He did not have a degree in History. He never taught in a History Department at a University. At Cambridge before the First World War he studied Classics. He later confessed that he had no interest in history at the time.[1] He did not take a Ph.D., nowadays the conventional route into the academic profession. On graduating in 1916, he went straight into the Foreign Office, where he remained for the next twenty years. During this time, he occupied his leisure, of which he seems to have had a great deal more than would be allowable nowadays, in writing biographical studies of nineteenth-century Russian writers and thinkers. He published a book on *Dostoevsky* in 1931, a study of Herzen and his circle (*The Romantic Exiles*) in 1933, and a biography of *Michael Bakunin* in 1937. He also began to write book reviews and articles on contemporary diplomacy. When in 1936 he resigned from the Foreign Office to take up a Chair at Aberystwyth University, it was to become Professor not of History but of International Relations.

In this guise, Carr became known for a number of short but influential works on foreign policy, most famously, perhaps, *The Twenty Years' Crisis 1919–1939*, published on the eve of the Second World War. Just as he had spent increasing amounts of time writing books while employed by the Foreign Office, however, so he now spent increasing amounts of time practising journalism while employed by the University. He became Assistant Editor of *The Times* in 1941 and wrote many leading articles for the newspaper until leaving his post in 1946. The fact that he was employed full-time by a national newspaper might not have endeared him to his employers at Aberystwyth, but it was because of his personal life that he was eventually obliged to resign his Chair. After a period of earning his living as a freelance journalist, lecturer and broadcaster, he obtained a Tutorship in Politics at Balliol College, Oxford, in 1953, before moving in 1955 to his final post, a Senior Research Fellowship at Trinity College, Cambridge, where he remained until his death in 1982 at the age of 90.[2]

Carr thus approached history from the angle of someone who had spent his life working for the Foreign Office and for a national newspaper. These influences and experiences strongly coloured his views about history and how it should be studied. He came to this subject relatively late in life. He embarked on his only major historical work, a *History of Soviet Russia*, published in fourteen volumes between 1950 and 1978, when he was in his fifties, and by the time he came to write *What is History?* he was already well past retirement age. He later claimed that his interest in history originated in the Russian Revolution itself, which he had viewed from afar as a junior clerk in the British Foreign Office in 1917. But it lay dormant for many years, until it was finally and decisively reawakened during the Second World War, when, like many others in Britain, though more thoroughly and permanently than most, he was converted to an admiration of – and preoccupation with – Soviet Russia on the entry of that country into the war as an ally of Britain in June 1941.[3]

Working on his *History of Soviet Russia* confronted Carr, as he said, with key questions such as 'Causation and Chance, Free Will and Determinism, the Individual and Society, Subjectivity and Objectivity' in what was to him a new field of intellectual endeavour. As a student he had been taught by 'a rather undistinguished classics don' at Cambridge that Herodotus' account of the Persian Wars was shaped and moulded by his attitude to the Peloponnesian War, which was in progress while he wrote. 'This was a fascinating revelation', Carr wrote many years later, 'and gave me my first understanding of what history was about.'[4] As he researched and wrote his study of Soviet Russia, Carr took up this insight and attempted to grapple with the theoretical problems which his project posed, in a series of articles written for *The Times Literary Supplement* in the course of the 1950s. The first of these was the question of objectivity. This was particularly important to him in view of the fact that by the time he came to publish the first volume of his history, in 1950, opinion on the Soviet Union was completely polarized between Communists, who would brook no criticism of it, and portrayed everything in its development as justified and inevitable; and the Cold War warriors of the West, who saw Communism as a threat to human rights and democratic values no less severe than that posed earlier by Nazism, and damned the development of the Soviet Union as a disastrous aberration.

Carr's *History of Soviet Russia* was a pioneering attempt to reconstruct in detail what happened in Russia between 1917 and 1933 from the available sources. It was also a serious attempt at steering a course between the opposite poles of Cold War polemics and delivering an account that could be regarded as scholarly and objective. But how should objectivity be defined in such a situation? In 1950, as the first volume of his monumental work was being published, Carr proclaimed boldly: 'Objective history does not exist.' Yet at the same time, he argued in the first of his articles for the *TLS*, to try and attain it was far from being a futile enterprise: 'To assert that fallible human beings are too much entangled in circumstances of time and place to attain the absolute truth', he wrote, 'is not the same thing as to deny the existence of truth; such a denial destroys any possible criterion of judgment, and makes any approach to history as true or as false as any other.' Clearly, this view was unsatisfactory. So Carr opted for a position 'where it is possible to maintain that objective truth exists, but that no historian by himself or no school of historian by itself, can hope to achieve more than a faint and partial approximation to it.'[5]

However, the problem was not so easily solved as that. In a review of the eminent diplomatic historian G. P. Gooch's *History and Historians in the Nineteenth Century*, a book first published in 1913 and reissued with a new Preface forty years later, Carr noted its 'unflagging faith in the possibility of establishing the facts and in the value to humanity of the facts, once established.' Such faith was a product of Gooch's training in the German historicist tradition of the nineteenth-century scholar Leopold von Ranke, in which the historian was taught to portray the past 'as it really was'. Yet the Gooch of 1952, continued Carr,

knows that the world has moved far in the past forty years, and that it is no longer possible for the present generation to accept this absolute and unqualified faith in the pre-eminence and in the saving grace of historical facts. . . . It will no longer be questioned that our search for the facts of history, and our identification of those facts when found, are necessarily determined by the – perhaps unconscious – beliefs and presuppositions which guide the search. The very conviction that 'facts' are neutral, and that progress consists in discovering the facts and learning lessons from them, is the product of a rational–liberal outlook on the world which cannot be so easily taken for granted to-day as it was by our more fortunately placed nineteenth-century ancestors.

At the same time, however, Carr conceded that the distortion of history by the Stalin regime in the Soviet Union, and its mutilation of documents and doctoring of the historical record, meant that freedom to know was more important than ever.[6]

Carr returned to the unresolved tensions evident in this article a few months later and tried to drive his thinking a few steps forward. What was the relationship between the historian and the facts? – he asked in another *TLS* article, published in June 1953:

> There is a two-way traffic between past and present, the present being moulded out of the past, yet constantly re-creating the past. If the historian makes history, it is equally true that history has made the historian. . . . The present-day philosopher of history, balancing uneasily on the razor edge between the hazards of objective determinism and the bottomless pit of subjective relativity, conscious that thought and action are inextricably intertwined, and that the nature of causation, in history no less than in science, seems the further to elude his grasp the more firmly he tries to grapple with it, is engaged in asking questions rather than in answering them.[7]

Some of these views were to resurface in *What is History?* But Carr could not really have believed that historians were only engaged in asking questions, since his *History of Soviet Russia* was answering them on almost every page. The problem thus remained unresolved.

In 1960 he had another go at the problem of objectivity in a discussion of nationalistic bias in history textbooks.

Here he was in a more paradoxical mood:

> The awkward thing about history is that bias seems an
> essential element in it – even in the best of history. The
> fact is that the facts do not, as is sometimes said, 'speak
> for themselves', or if they do it is the historian who
> decides which facts shall speak – he cannot give the floor
> to them all. And the decision of the most conscientious
> historian – of the historian most conscious of what he is
> doing – will be determined by a point of view which
> others may call biased. It would not be altogether cynical
> to say that the best historian is the historian with the best
> bias – not the non-existent historian with no bias at all.

From Carr's point of view, the best bias in this case was an
international rather than a national bias, which meant abandoning the writing of history as an act of patriotism, such as
had been undertaken by German historians in their discussions of the Treaty of Versailles and its consequences, and
taking a view that saw the recent past of Germany and its
place in the international system since 1919 from the point
of view of the international system itself. Whether 'bias' was
really the right word for this must, however, be doubted.
What Carr really seemed to be saying was that German historians in recent years had begun to be *less* biased because
they were beginning to see beyond their country's own
narrow national interest when they examined its past. 'One
may reasonably ask of the historian', Carr concluded, 'that
he should march at the head of the progressive and enlightened movements of his time, and not lag behind them.'[8]
Yet who was to say what was progressive and enlightened
and what was not? Here too Carr did not seem to have
resolved the problem of objectivity in any satisfactory way.
He was clearly torn between the feeling that objectivity was
under threat amidst the polemics of the Cold War, and the

belief that objectivity in any traditional sense of the word was an impossible ambition that no historian could reasonably hope to attain. These tensions in Carr's thinking were to surface in a rather different way at the beginning of the 1960s when he attempted to pull all these strands of thought together in *What is History?*.[9]

## II

'History', Carr wrote in a review published in 1954, 'would not be worth writing or reading if it had no meaning.' It was crucial in his view to challenge the 'assumption that the important explanations in history are to be found in the conscious purposes and foresights of the *dramatis personae*'.[10] But where did the meaning in history come from? Here Carr worked out his ideas in the course of a long controversy with the philosopher and historian of ideas Isaiah Berlin, a friend with whom he was on intimate enough terms for the two to address each other, unusually by the standards of the day, by their first names. The two men shared a profound knowledge of and interest in Russian literature and thought. Both were heavily influenced in their political thinking by the English liberal tradition. But on the Soviet Union they parted company. While he was far from uncritical of many aspects of the Communist regime in Russia, Carr never entirely lost the sympathy which it had generated in him during its struggle against Hitler in the Second World War. Berlin, on the other hand, as a refugee from Soviet Russia, had no such sympathy. He became in the course of the 1950s one of the main spokesmen for liberal, 'Western' values and against Communist theory and ideology on both sides of the Atlantic.[11]

In 1950, Berlin reviewed the first volume of Carr's *History of Soviet Russia* in terms that left no doubt about his disagreement with its method and its thrust. Carr had written in the book's Preface that his intention was 'to write the history not of the events of the revolution . . . but of the political, social and economic order which emerged from it.' Thus his book aimed to provide 'not an exhaustive record of the events of the period to which it relates, but an analysis of those events which moulded the main lines of development.'[12] So for example he traced in minute detail the development of Bolshevik thinking on a whole range of topics before 1917, even though the Bolsheviks were of little or no political importance in Russia at the time, because this thinking was crucial in moulding the policies the Bolsheviks put into effect after they came to power. On the other hand, he left out any consideration of the events of the revolution, the defeated alternatives to the Bolsheviks, or the barbarous conflict of the Civil War.

For Carr, writing from the perspective of a long-serving Foreign Office mandarin, what was important was the process of state-building and the moulding of state policy. And like many civil servants, he took state-generated documents, formal policies, constitutions and paper legislation very much at face value. As Carr's biographer Jonathan Haslam has noted, his experience as a diplomat had 'cut short the sense that there could be a multitude of possible outcomes to any situation; once an event had occurred, whether it was good or bad, the diplomat accepted it and moved on'. And it had 'underscored his identification with rulers rather than ruled . . . in writing the *History* Carr subconsciously transposed his early identification with the ruling class in Britain to the ruling caste in Soviet Russia.'[13]

Berlin found this procedure fundamentally objectionable. Carr, he complained in his review of the book, 'sees history as a procession of events ruled by inexorable laws'. Carr seemed to think that the task of the historian consisted in making clear what these laws were and how they operated, 'without so much as a background glance at unrealized possibilities upon which great hopes and fears had once been focused, still less upon the victims and casualties of the process.' Thus Carr, he charged,

> sees history through the eyes of the victors; the losers have for him all but disqualified themselves from bearing witness. . . . If Mr. Carr's remaining volumes equal this impressive opening they will constitute the most monumental challenge of our time to that ideal of impartiality and objective truth and even-handed justice in the writing of history which is most deeply embedded in the European liberal tradition.[14]

For Berlin, therefore, Carr's approach to history was anything but objective. Carr may have thought that if he did have a bias, it was the best bias. Berlin obviously disagreed.

Berlin expanded on his view of history in 1953, continuing his attack on Carr in a more implicit way. His biographer Michael Ignatieff has described Berlin's Auguste Comte Lecture of that year, delivered at the London School of Economics, as 'an impressive statement of his most fundamental beliefs'. Human beings, argued Berlin in this lecture, later published in an expanded form under the title *Historical Inevitability*, were unique in their capacity for moral choice, which rendered them relatively independent of the impersonal forces which historians like Carr, wrongly in Berlin's view, saw as determining human behaviour. Of course, Berlin conceded, such forces did constrain the room for manoeuvre of individual humans in any given situation. It was the historian's job to work out what that room for manoeuvre was, to identify possible alternative courses of action to the ones individuals eventually took, and to judge their behaviour accordingly. To insist on the inevitability of what had happened in the past, as Carr did, was to resign moral responsibility for our own actions in the present.[15]

Carr was not one to take such criticism lying down. In a review of the lecture in the *TLS*, he insisted that 'the specific function of the historian, *qua* historian, is not to judge but to explain'. Historians, as even Berlin had conceded, had always looked for meaning and pattern in the past.

> The annalist is content to say that one thing followed another; what distinguishes the historian is the proposition that one thing led to another. Secondly, while historical events were of course set in motion by the individual wills, whether of 'great men' or of ordinary people, the historian must go behind the individual wills and inquire into the reasons which made the individuals will and act as they did, and study the 'factors' or 'forces' which explain individual behaviour. Thirdly, while history never repeats itself, it presents certain regularities, and permits of certain generalizations, which can serve as a guide to future action.[16]

It was these arguments that lay behind Carr's assault on Berlin's views in the pages of *What is History?*.

When the managers of the Trevelyan Fund, created by the great Cambridge historian G. M. Trevelyan from the profits of his immensely successful *English Social History* and from his considerable private wealth, asked Carr to deliver the second set of Trevelyan Lectures in 1961, following on the inaugural series delivered by A. L. Rowse, they were helping to establish a tradition whereby the Trevelyan lecturer is normally a figure from outside the Cambridge History Faculty but enjoys some past or present connection with it. Carr fitted the bill perfectly: he had never been a member of the History Faculty at Cambridge, but he was a graduate of the University and a Fellow – soon to be a Life Fellow – of

Trinity College, which in the curiously bifurcated structure of Cambridge meant that he was a member of a self-governing College of considerable wealth and prestige but not an employee of the University itself. He could supervise research students, and did, and he was entitled to supervise undergraduates, but he was not part of the normal lecturing staff of the History Faculty. Apart from anything else, by the time he gave the Trevelyan Lectures he was, at nearly seventy, well past retirement age.

In asking Carr to deliver the lectures, the Managers of the Trevelyan Fund were hoping that he would talk about Soviet Russia, a topic which was not at that time taught in the History Faculty, where the syllabus still concentrated overwhelmingly on the course of English history from the early Middle Ages onwards. But Carr had different ideas. As he wrote to his friend Isaac Deutscher, the biographer of Stalin and Trotsky, in March 1960, 'I have been looking for some time for an opportunity to deliver a broadside on history in general' and 'to answer, among other things, the foolish remarks of Popper, Isaiah Berlin etc. about history'.[17] In *What is History?*, he did as much as he promised, and more. He drafted the lectures during a sea-voyage from London to San Francisco between 10 September and 11 October 1959 and redrafted them a year later, beginning on 27 September 1960. The lectures were delivered week by week in Cambridge from January to March 1961, repeated on BBC radio and printed in abridged form in the BBC's weekly magazine *The Listener.* They were probably more widely publicized than any set of Trevelyan Lectures before or since.[18]

As a journalist with many media connections, Carr had instant access to the BBC. Given his clear intention of securing them the widest possible publicity, he wrote the lectures in his journalistic mode, using all the skills he had honed to perfection over many years of writing for the newspapers. It is clear that from the outset they were addressed to a much broader audience than those who were gathered at the Mill Lane lecture in Cambridge. Carr brought in Isaiah Berlin not just because of the ongoing debate between the two, but also because he knew that listeners would be familiar with his name. Both men were well known figures in the public intellectual life of their time. Both were frequent broadcasters on the radio, the most popular broadcast medium of the 1950s, not yet overtaken by television and, some would argue, better suited to the transmission and discussion of sophisticated arguments and ideas. The intellectual world of Britain at the beginning of the 1960s was still very intimate; only a tiny proportion of the population had ever studied at university, the historical profession was still small enough for most historians to know each other on personal terms; and intellectual debate in the media, including *The Times*, the BBC's Third Programme and the *TLS*, was still dominated by a select group of public figures, a group to which both Berlin and Carr belonged. An outside observer remarked on 'the smallness of English intellectual society, the availability of space in newspapers and periodicals of the better class (indeed, their encouragement of controversial material), [and] the highly individual and belligerent nature of English scholars' as influences which imparted a rare coherence to English intellectual life and gave it a particular penchant for public debate.[19]

As Carr's lectures were published in *The Listener*, therefore, they inevitably aroused comment in the magazine's correspondence columns. Isaiah Berlin in particular was quick to respond to the barbs fired at him by his Cambridge friend. Berlin claimed that he had been misrepresented in the lectures. He had not said that determinism was false; he had merely said that it was a fallacy to make impersonal forces responsible for what men had done. Nor had he argued that it was wrong to search for the causes of human action, a point on which Carr certainly caricatured his position in the lectures.[20] Carr responded by quoting from *Historical Inevitability* to the effect that if Berlin thought that determinism was incompatible with individual responsibility, then he must believe that determinism was false. And if Berlin considered it wrong not to heap moral praise or blame on individuals in the past, then he must consider it right to judge them morally.[21]

Berlin replied to Carr repeating the charge of misrepresentation. At the same time, he reiterated his view that the arguments for determinism were unconvincing:

> The determinist proposition that individual (or indeed any) actions are wholly determined by identifiable causes in time is not compatible with belief in individual responsibility. . . . I see no reason for denying that men have a limited freedom of individual action, but within conditions that are largely not of their own choosing.[22]

This last phrase lightly paraphrased a famous dictum to the same effect by Karl Marx, the subject of biographical studies by both Berlin and Carr in the 1930s.[23] It was in fact saying no more than Berlin had said in his *Historical Inevitability*. Carr found himself in difficulties trying to justify his misrepresentation of Berlin on this point and was forced to concede, in a private letter to his friend written on 27 June 1961, that he 'probably overstated my case', perhaps because he was oversensitive to the charge of a crude determinism in his work as a result of attacks on his *History of Soviet Russia* by Cold War warriors. Nevertheless, he insisted that Berlin's arguments still tended in the direction of denying the validity of determinism and asserting the necessity of moral judgment in history.[24] Berlin's response was to say that he only admitted that moral judgment was permissible for the historian; he did not claim that it was a duty.[25] The two men's positions seemed to be moving closer together.

However, Berlin did not give up his attack on Carr. In another private letter, written on 3 July 1961, he suggested that most historians actually did engage in moral judgment. He cited Carr's account of Lenin as an example – his characterization of Lenin as progressive surely implied moral approbation, just as his description of other individuals as reactionary implied the reverse. He asked Carr to acknowledge in the published version of the lectures that he was satisfied that Berlin did not hold all the views that *What is History?* claimed he did. But Carr refused, saying that the publishing process had gone too far and it was too late.[26] This opened the way for a resumption of hostilities on a larger scale.

## III

On 5 January 1962, Berlin reviewed *What is History?* for the *New Statesman* magazine. Here, rather than reopening the debate over what he regarded as Carr's misrepresentation of his own views, he launched a wider attack on some of Carr's central theses. Carr argued that theory had to be used in explaining the past, and that describing the conscious motives and desires of the actors in history was not enough by itself to account for what they did. But surely, asked Berlin, Lenin's conscious motives and desires were important factors in the Bolshevik revolution? Surely, if Stalin had died before Lenin, the subsequent course of Soviet history would have been different?[27] In similar vein, a review of *What is History?* in the *TLS* by Isaac Deutscher asked: 'If accident does [as Carr claimed] modify the course of events yet does not modify the historian's "hierarchy of significant causes", is there not something wrong with that hierarchy?'[28] Carr came in the course of time to concede that there was something in this argument. 'The word "accident"', he wrote to Isaac Deutscher in 1963, 'is unfortunate':

Lenin's death was not strictly speaking an accident. It had no doubt perfectly definite causes. But these belong to medicine, and not to historical study. But it seems to me difficult to say that these causes, though extraneous to History, did not affect its course. Even if you maintain that in the long run everything would have turned out much the same, there is a short run which is important, and makes a great deal of difference to a great many people. . . . Of course, if History . . . were nothing but a succession of extraneous 'accidents', it could not be a serious study at all. But it is in fact subject to sufficient regularities to make it a serious study, though these regularities are from time to time interrupted or upset by extraneous elements.[29]

Later on, in an interview with Perry Anderson, editor of *New Left Review*, to mark the completion of his *History of Soviet Russia*, Carr modified his views on this point still further. Lenin, he insisted, would still have thrown the Soviet Union into headlong industrialization and collectivization had he lived. But he would never have falsified historical writing to the extent that Stalin did, and he would have tried to 'minimize and mitigate the element of coercion', unlike Stalin, who maximized it. This may have been too rosy a view of Lenin. But it did concede that personality had some influence on the way things happened, though Carr still insisted that it had little influence on the overall trend of development.[30]

Carr's account of causation was unsatisfactory in other ways too. As W. H. Walsh, author of a widely used text on the philosophy of history, commented: 'His whole discussion of causation . . . is marred by his failure to ask whether the search for causes in history is practical or theoretical.'[31] This was fundamentally because Carr's formative intellectual years were spent not in the ivory tower of academia but in the practical world of the diplomatic service and the

Foreign Office, where nothing was of direct interest unless it made a contribution to the formation of policy. Carr could never free himself from the assumption that history was primarily designed to provide a guide to policy. But, A. J. P. Taylor asked, 'why should knowledge of where I came from tell me where I am going to?'[32] The medievalist Geoffrey Barraclough, whose war service had converted him to the view that it was more important to study contemporary history, made the same basic point at greater length:

> It seems sometimes as though Mr. Carr is perilously near to the doctrine that history exists to fulfil a social need. If so, he is confusing history and myth. What society calls for – and too often gets – is not history but myth, the cement which holds all society together. Precisely because, as Mr. Carr urges, history is rational, it is essentially personal and anti-social.[33]

Barraclough was echoing a widely held view that the function of historians was to puncture myths, not create them.

Carr's argument in *What is History?* that the only causes that were of interest to the historian were the causes which could be of use in formulating policy for the future was one of the weakest in the book. Historians investigate causes in order to explain what happened, and while Carr was surely right to maintain that wider causes and contexts are essential to such an explanation, there was no intellectual justification for his suggestion that any causes, wider or not, that were of no use as a guide to future action should be ignored: that was the way to precisely the kind of manipulation of history in the interests of politics that he so roundly condemned in Stalin and his followers.[34]

As a participant in the negotiation of the 1919 Peace Settlement, one of the most disastrous international agreements of modern times, Carr might also have realized that when people do learn lessons from history, they often learn the wrong ones. History is a very poor predictor of future developments and future events. In attempting to rescue the notion of history's predictive capabilities from its detractors, Carr confused historical laws with historical generalizations. Scientific laws do not merely assert that there is a pattern with a few exceptions: they predict precisely and with a premiss of inevitability, so that when two particular chemicals are put together in a crucible, for example, they will always and inevitably react in a particular way. All that historians can do is to generalize and attempt to find patterns that make a reasonable fit with the historical evidence; but they cannot use these generalizations and patterns to predict the future, because there will always be exceptions to them. Moreover, the larger the generalization, the more exceptions there are likely to be. Historians use hypotheses, as Carr agreed, such as Max Weber's famous idea that there was a connection between Protestantism and the rise of capitalism; but they never expect them to be wholly confirmed when they pit them against the historical evidence. Thus they can never be laws.

The process of writing and research was in Carr's view one of continuous interaction between hypotheses and evidence. His account of the process of research and writing as simultaneous rather than sequential was to some extent a reflection of his own personal habits. It has often been described how he would occupy a chair in his sitting-room, surrounded by scraps and sheets of paper that would accumulate around it as he put his thoughts down and began to stitch them together.[35] Anyone who wants to get an idea of just how disorderly this seemed only has to open the folders of notes for the never-completed second edition of *What is History?* in the Carr papers at Birmingham University Library, with their seemingly random scribblings on pieces of paper of varying sizes, all in no obvious order. In the age of the word-processor this seems very primitive; nor does it bear much apparent resemblance to the orderly working habits of, say, the great historian Edward Gibbon, who would pace up and down in his room composing each paragraph in his head until it was ready to put down on paper, word-perfect and never to be altered again. Nevertheless, it does not seem to have been all that unusual. One eminent historian, Sir Llewellyn Woodward, wrote to Carr describing how

> I too have always started to write as soon as I have read – from what you call the capital sources – a certain necessary minimum about a subject, and I too have begun nearly always in the middle or the end, without having an ordered plan or a full sheaf of notes. In my innocence I have regarded this as a shameful thing on my part, and I have assumed that no historian worth the name worked as I work – a kind of headlong and excited muddle – continually adding to and altering drafts, and changing my opinions as I read more. It is an immense relief to find that a proper historian like yourself does as I do.[36]

Though both historians were probably more disorganized in their writing habits than most, the general principle described by Carr, of research and writing forming a continuously interactive process, at least after the initial period of exploration in the libraries and archives is over, is probably one that most historians would recognize, and has a great deal to recommend it.

## IV

Berlin's critique of Carr's concept of causation and his insistence on the importance of historical context led on to what was perhaps the most important aspect of his disagreement with Carr, namely Carr's concept of objectivity. Objectivity, according to Berlin, could be found in the historian's method; it was not a question of the historian's interpretation. The test of objective methods was 'whether their results can be checked by observation, not of one observer but of many, whether the logic of the arguments is internally consistent, whether they are accepted widely enough by those whose own claims to expertise can themselves be tested empirically.' By these criteria, he went on, the liberal-conservative French historian Halévy and his Russian counterpart Klyuchevsky, whose sympathies were with the defeated Tsarist regime rather than with its Bolshevik successor, were objective, while the American progressive Beard and the Soviet historian Pokrovsky were not, despite their identification with the forces of change. Yet Carr equated progressiveness with objectivity. His definition of an objective historian was one who had 'the capacity to project his vision into the future in such a way as to give him a more profound and more lasting insight into the past than can be attained by those historians whose outlook is entirely bounded by their own immediate situation'.[37] But, as one critic put it:

> After the future has become the past the question of whether this or that historian did have the future in his bones may not necessarily be decided more correctly than it would be decided here and now by the historian's contemporaries. The question might be decided differently at different times in the future by different sets of judges with different questions to ask and different ends to serve.[38]

Put more simply, it was more than likely that the historian's vision of the future would be falsified by events, as indeed Carr's own vision of a future organized along the lines of a Soviet-style planned economy, modified no doubt in a social-democratic direction, has proved so far to be. Carr could not, and did not, envisage the collapse of Communism and the end of the Soviet Union, events which falsified his view of objectivity as the analysis of the past in conformity with a quasi-Marxist vision of the future.

There was in Berlin's view a second flaw in Carr's concept of objectivity, and that lay in his definition of progress. In Carr's estimation, he charged, 'whatever occurs is good because it occurs – we know the stages we have passed to have been the right goals only because they have been realised.' Progress was 'whatever those in power will in fact achieve'. Carr was always on the side of the big battalions.[39] This point was taken up by other reviewers, notably by H. R. Trevor-Roper, then Regius Professor of Modern History at Oxford University and a noted polemicist against the left. For Carr, Trevor-Roper charged,

'objectivity' means, not being 'objective' in the hitherto accepted sense of the word – i.e., being uncommitted, dispassionate, fair – but the exact opposite, being committed to that side which is going to win: to the big battalions. . . . What is the most obvious characteristic of *A History of Soviet Russia*? It is the author's unhesitating identification of history with the victorious cause, his ruthless dismissal of its opponents, of its victims, and of all who did not stay on, or steer, the bandwaggon. The 'might-have-beens', the deviationists, the rivals, the critics of Lenin are reduced to insignificance, denied justice, or hearing, or space, because they backed the wrong horse. History proved them wrong, and the historian's essential task is to take the side of History. Those whom History found wanting as politicians may not be heard even as witnesses of fact, even in order to be condemned. Whatever they believed, whatever they saw, whatever they said is ignored as irrelevant, their voices are silenced, and silenced with contempt. No historian since the crudest ages of clerical bigotry has treated evidence with such dogmatic ruthlessness as this. No historian, even in those ages, has exalted such dogmatism into an historiographical theory.

Carr's 'vulgar worship of success' had been evident in the 1930s, noted Trevor-Roper, in his championing of the appeasement of Hitler's Germany; now he had transferred it to Stalin's Russia.[40]

Trevor-Roper's attack was by far the most savage of all those directed from various quarters at *What is History?*. As one commentator noted, he 'had a gift for marshalling the faults of a historian' but did so 'without a grain of sympathy. After reading him, one wondered why the books had been written at all, why anyone read them, why anyone took them seriously.' In his hands, criticism did not lead to 'an enhancement of our understanding'; it was simply 'an instrument of destruction'.[41] Yet whatever the polemical excesses of his style, Trevor-Roper had raised an important point. Other reviewers, even those whose politics normally placed them on the left, also commented that Carr 'tends to accept that what has happened is historically right'.[42] Change, as A. J. P. Taylor pointed out, was not necessarily the same as progress:

> Stalin's extermination of the kulaks was justified because it helped to produce what has happened, that is, the present strength of the Soviet Union. (By analogy, though Mr. Carr does not say so, Hitler's extermination of the Jews was not justified because Germany now is not a world Power). . . . How can the fact that something happened prove it right or, for that matter, wrong?[43]

There was a good deal in these criticisms. Taylor was making the point, in effect, that Carr's rigorous exclusion of moral judgment from history was exercised in favour of the powerful, the victors of history, and those who had run roughshod over the masses in the name of progress. This was ironic in the light of the fact that Carr's early writings had been devoted to some of history's most spectacular losers, such as the Russian populist Herzen, who spent most of his life in exile, or the anarchist Bakunin, whose many revolutionary escapades in various parts of Europe were a long litany of failure and humiliation. What would happen if the Soviet Union, which appeared in the early 1960s to be rivalling the United States in wealth and power, were to collapse in the way that Nazi Germany had done? Would this suddenly render the extermination of the kulaks morally unjustifiable?

Carr took all these criticisms with a pinch of salt. He told an interviewer that he felt 'insulted' that Trevor-Roper had 'let him off so lightly'. It was disappointing because it was a 'bad polemic'. Neither Trevor-Roper nor Berlin had any vision of the future; both of them looked back to some Golden Age in the past, though where Trevor-Roper located it was difficult to say 'because he hasn't written enough to give himself away even on that'.[44] Carr thought that good historians would rise above the limitations of their own time not merely by projecting themselves into an imagined future, however, but also, perhaps more reasonably, by recognizing the nature and extent of their own prejudices. There was something in this suggestion. Certainly historians will write better history if they are self-conscious about their political and intellectual starting-point. Carr thought, however, that historians could not escape the influence of their own time. This introduced an important contradiction into his argument. As A. J. P. Taylor remarked:

> The general principle that each age gets the historians it deserves does not work out in practice or works so hap-

hazardly as to be no principle at all. The present day in England, when the educated classes have lost faith in the future and in themselves, no doubt deserves conservative historians, as Mr. Carr suggests. . . . How then does our disillusioned age come to deserve Mr. Carr, or even me?[45]

Carr did not find this point difficult to answer: 'Different types of historians', he said, 'people with different shades of opinion, can emerge from the same society because of personal factors – their home environment, school and college, and so on.' What he was trying to explain were general tendencies, not individual peculiarities.[46]

Other critics made the point that what appeared to be a tendency in *What is History?* to argue that all history was subjective, was contradicted by the style and content of *A History of Soviet Russia*, which was objective and empirical almost to a fault.[47] Carr's biographer Jonathan Haslam, indeed, has noted 'a curious divorce between his reflections on the nature of the subject and the manner in which he practised his profession'. Carr himself virtually admitted the existence of such a disjuncture when responding to the criticism that his view of history left no room for losers, to whom he had devoted almost no attention in the *History of Soviet Russia*. 'That is the fault of my History', he replied, 'not of my theory of history.'[48] Yet this disjuncture was in many ways more a matter of style than of substance. *What is History?* belongs essentially with Carr's journalism, as its careful preparation for broadcasting on the radio and printing in *The Listener* suggests. That indeed is why, in contradistinction to large swathes of *A History of Soviet Russia*, it is so readable and entertaining. But despite appearing on occasion to be so, Carr was not an advocate of unbridled relativism in *What is History?*, while *A History of Soviet Russia*, for all the dense empiricism of its detail, was cast in a mould that Isaiah Berlin for one considered biased in the extreme. As

Jonathan Haslam has remarked, the thawing of the Cold War meant that Carr felt less of an obligation in 1961 than he had done in more embattled times, ten years or so earlier, in his articles for the *TLS*, to stand up for the traditional liberal historian's belief in 'the sanctity of facts'.[49] But the essential point was that he still believed, at bottom, in the desirability of historians rising above the subjectivities of their own time, and in their capacity to do so, even if the way in which he expressed this belief was rightly criticized by some as being itself highly subjective.

Nevertheless, Carr's suggestion, nowadays part of the basic conceptual equipment of the historical profession, that all historians carried some kind of personal conceptual, intellectual and political baggage with them when they went into the archive, and his warning that the sources which they used had their own biases too, outraged the more conservative members of the historical establishment in his own day. Very few English historians had given much thought to the issues he raised in *What is History?* G. M. Trevelyan, who was a very old man by the time Carr gave the lectures, was not untypical. He wrote to Carr to tell him that he had had his lectures read to him one a week in his home. Apparently forgetting that one series had already been given by A. L. Rowse, Trevelyan expressed his gratitude to Carr 'that you have given that course of lectures which is called after me such a good start'. But, he added: 'I read Hegel's *Philosophy of History* between sixty and seventy years ago and thought it such poor stuff that I never troubled myself any more with the theory of history but only practised it.'[50]

Views such as these were common in the Cambridge History Faculty. Privately, Carr considered the Faculty a 'not very distinguished historical community'.[51] He devoted some attention in *What is History?* to attacking one of its leading figures, Herbert Butterfield, holder of the Chair of Modern History, for which Carr himself had been passed over some years before. At the time, Butterfield's *The Whig Interpretation of History*, published in 1931, was regarded as an important book and was set reading for undergraduates. It was among other things a diatribe against historians who allowed their present-day beliefs to mould their interpretation of the past. Carr pointed out in his lectures that Butterfield had done just that in his later works. But his attack on the Cambridge History Faculty went much further. Underlining the fact that he had never been a member of the Faculty himself, Carr said he was 'told' that there were no lectures given by members of the Faculty on Russian or Chinese history, for example. He called for a reform of the undergraduate teaching curriculum to broaden it out from its existing focus on English history from the Middle Ages onwards.[52]

Carr met with some sympathy for these views among some members of the Faculty. His lectures proved the catalyst for a major attempt to reform the curriculum by abandoning the insistence on compulsory English history and including a wider element of choice, including a strong dose of extra-European history. Carr himself advised on these proposals, but they met with stiff opposition, and even after a modified version of them had been agreed by the Faculty, their opponents mounted a partially successful rearguard action in the Senate. Nevertheless, the mould was broken; compulsory English history from early medieval times onwards was dropped as a requirement in the curriculum, and the way was open for the gradual changes which, some four decades later, have made social history, Indian and African history, gender history and cultural history vital aspects of the undergraduate history course at Cambridge. Similar moves were afoot in Oxford, and Carr's work was taken as a signal by young radicals there such as the Marxist historian T. W. Mason, who used a review of *What is History?* to thunder against 'the ponderous anachronism of continuous English history' in the undergraduate curriculum at Oxford, and to launch a History Reform Group, which, Oxford being Oxford, was still in existence a decade later without having made any meaningful progress in the meantime.[53]

V

By the time the Cambridge curriculum reform proposals reached the Senate, five years had elapsed. Shortly afterwards, the leading objector to Carr's views, the Tudor historian G. R. Elton, put his objections together in a counterblast entitled *The Practice of History*, published in 1967. Encouraged by his publisher, Elton attacked Carr's *What is History?* in the strongest terms in his book, inveighing against his championing of extra-European history, his contention that history had a purpose and a meaning, and above all his view that historians carried their own ideas and preconceptions into their work, a view he described as 'pernicious nonsense' leading to an 'extreme relativism' which made 'the historian the creator of history'.[54] Elton was exaggerating here, of course; no dispassionate reader of *What is History?* could possibly avoid noticing that Carr believed first, that historians should try to rise above their personal prejudices when writing history, and second, that the evidence and the materials with which historians worked imposed their own limitations on what it was possible for them to say. Historical research in his view was an interaction between the historian and the materials, not a one-way traffic in which the historian was active and the materials passive. If Carr was a relativist, then it was certainly not of any variety that could reasonably be called extreme. Elton argued forcefully that the historian had to listen to the sources and avoid importing any ideas into them from the present; but this was extremism in the opposite direction, and left unanswered the key question of how historians were to select the documents with which they worked and the topics which they studied, a question to which Elton himself never provided a satisfactory answer.[55]

A more telling criticism of Carr's position was that he gave too much weight to the historian in deciding what was a historical fact. The example Carr chose in *What is History?* was the killing of a gingerbread salesman at a fair by a drunken mob in the early Victorian era. This had been, he said, turned into a historical fact by virtue of being mentioned in a book by Carr's colleague at Trinity College, George Kitson Clark. The example was perhaps unfortunate, since a subsequent investigation of the incident established that there was no reference to any such occurrence in contemporary sources. These emphasized on the contrary the remarkable lack of drunken violence at the fair in question. Carr was insufficiently critical of Kitson Clark's use in this instance of a highly dubious source, the later memoirs of the circus-owner 'Lord' George Sanger.[56] So there was very little evidence that what Carr was referring to was a fact of any kind at all. Nevertheless, it was reasonable to claim that had it actually occurred, its factuality was independent of any process of cognition on the part of historians.

The *TLS* reviewer (Isaac Deutscher) took up this point. The extermination of millions of Jews by the Nazis was a historical fact regardless of whether historians wrote about it or not, and pointed out that Carr in effect conceded this when he used the analogy of the mountain. 'It does not follow', Carr wrote, 'that because a mountain appears to take on different shapes from different angles of vision, it has objectively either no shape at all or an infinity of shapes.' What did follow, Deutscher went on to suggest, was that the mountain had a shape that was in reality independent of the way it was seen by its observers. And Carr himself accepted this. The historian, he went on to say, has to respect the facts, not merely in terms of accuracy, but also in terms of bringing into the picture all knowable facts that were relevant to the subject and the argument. One of the commonest accusations levelled at Carr by his conservative opponents, that of total relativism, was thus very wide of the mark.[57]

But how could the historian decide what facts to put in and what to leave out? Carr thought that it was better to decide by the self-conscious use of theory rather than by mobilising unconscious prejudices in the way that Elton, a strong conservative in every sense of the word, did in his own work on Tudor government. But there were limits to Carr's enthusiasm for sociological theory. He wrote to the economic historian M. M. Postan some years later:

> I recognise that many present-day historians are dead because they have no theory. But the theory which they lack is a theory of history, not one delivered from outside. What is needed is a two-way traffic. I do not need to tell you what the historian must learn from the economic, demographic, military etc. etc. specialist. But the economist, demographer etc. etc. will also die unless he works within a broader historical pattern which only the 'general' historian can provide. The trouble is, as I said before, that historical theories are by their nature theories of change, and that we live in the society which wants or reluctantly accepts only subsidiary or 'specialized' changes in a stabilized historical equilibrium. Hence the flight from history into 'sectoral specialization'.[58]

By this time, to judge from the folders of notes and clippings he kept for a possible second edition of *What is History?*, Carr had moved far closer to a Marxist position than he had been in 1961.[59] What he meant by a 'theory of history' was thus most probably Marxism. Yet whatever theories he thought were the right ones, he never used them in his own work in any explicit way. Although he argued that economic and social factors were decisive in history, they barely made an appearance in his *History of Soviet Russia* as determinants of political change. He may have described the Bolshevik Revolution as a popular revolution, driven from below, but he was not really interested in analysing how or why this was so.

What interested him was, ironically, the same thing that interested Elton, namely the operation of government and administration. At bottom, both shared an elitist view of history. Nowhere did Carr's elitism, his identification with the government rather than the governed, come out more strongly than in his dismissal not only of the losers in history but also of the vast majority of human beings throughout recorded time as being uninteresting to the historian because they had contributed nothing to the process of historical change. 'Surely', one critic protested, 'historians do not forfeit their titles or abandon their offices when they concentrate on the politically and economically powerless or on the defeated.'[60] Yet Carr dismissed the Russian peasantry, for example, as 'a primitive, cunning, ignorant and brutish lot' and insisted that 'the original design' of the Soviet 'regime – to educate the peasants to mechanise and modernise and organise agriculture – was perfectly sensible and enlightened': it was simply too utopian given the small numbers and poor quality of the men sent to enforce it, and led to violence on a tragic scale 'when they came up against peasant stupidity and peasant obstinacy'.[61]

This rather mandarin view of the common people was quickly to become outdated, as historians from the mid-1960s onwards turned their attention to rescuing the poor and the dispossessed in history 'from the enormous condescension of posterity', to quote the famous phrase used in E. P. Thompson's *The Making of the English Working Class*, published just two years after Carr's lectures, in 1963. *What is History?* indeed was written on the eve of a revolution in British historical scholarship. This was proclaimed above all in three special issues of the *TLS* in 1966, where articles by a number of historians proclaimed the importance not only of extra-European history and social and economic history, but also the need to study the seemingly ignorant and deluded in the past, and to use modern social theory to explain their behaviour in rational terms.[62]

# VI

In some key respects, therefore, Carr's views have not stood the test of time. His teleologically instrumentalized concept of objectivity, his policy-oriented theory of causation, his Olympian disdain for the history of ordinary people, his unconscious identification with the governing rather than the governed, his sweeping and cavalier rejection of the role of the accidental and the contingent, his confusion of historical laws with historical generalizations, his dogmatic rejection of any element of moral judgment in history at all, his insistence that history had a meaning and a direction – none of these aspects of Carr's argument in *What is History?* has found much favour with subsequent historians.

Moreover, recently Carr's views have come under strong attack from another direction, namely from postmodernist hyper-relativists who believe he made too many concessions to the English empiricism which a number of reviewers saw as such a key influence on his book.[63] One postmodernist has condemned Carr as 'epistemologically conservative', a 'convinced objectivist' and the proponent of ideas and methods 'conducive to the empirical historical method'.[64] Another has excoriated Carr as a champion of 'objectivity and even truth', 'certaintist', 'unreflexive' and 'too naïve to be taken seriously today'.[65] This, as has been remarked, is 'the language of an eradication campaign'.[66] Certainly, as these critics have pointed out, there are contradictions in Carr's work, and undeniably in some respects it was already out of date, or soon to be so, as we have already seen. However, their depiction of Carr as an unregenerate empiricist is as distorted as Elton's portrayal of Carr as an out-and-out relativist. One of the things that makes the book so fascinating is precisely the tension between the two, a tension that Carr never in the end quite manages to resolve.

Where Carr has been overtaken by intellectual change has been, undeniably, in the area of language and textuality, the focus of a great deal of writing on history in the decades since he published his book. Yet this has not had the radically destructive effect on historical knowledge that many of its more extreme proponents claim, not least because of the implications of total relativism for their own work; for if everything really is subjective, if we can know nothing for sure about the past, and meaning is only put into texts by those who read them, then why should we believe what the postmodernists themselves are saying, and why should we not put into their texts a meaning that is the opposite of the one they intended?[67]

One of many developments in historical scholarship since Carr wrote has been the emergence of genres of history which carry a strong moral charge, from feminist history – and it is one of the aspects of Carr's style that most grates on the present-day reader that he persistently refers to 'the historian' as 'he' – to Holocaust history; and it is the latter that has done more than anything else, perhaps, to restore the notion of historical fact independent of the historian's recognition of it, in the course of its battle against the school of 'Holocaust deniers' who maintain that there were no Jews gassed at Auschwitz, no Nazi programme of extermination, no six million dead.[68] Carr's obdurate insistence on the illegitimacy of any kind of moral judgment in history simply will not stand up in the face of such topics, though historians would on the other hand do well to note his warnings that too many and too simplistic moral judgments are more likely to make the historian look ridiculous than to add anything to the reader's understanding of the subject under review.[69] Another recent and welcome development has been the turn of historians to the study of the irrational in the past, something which Carr either refused to recognize at all, at least in collectivities, or condemned out of hand when he was forced to admit it was there. Carr's optimistic faith in reason and progress seems indeed more than a little out of place amidst the more sober and chastened atmosphere of the early twenty-first century.

Yet for all its flaws, its inner contradictions and its outdated approach to many aspects of the study of history, *What is History?* remains a classic. It has, after all, sold over a quarter of a million copies since its first publication, and with good reason. Like many books that were written quickly and originated in lectures, it has a fluent and pungent style that is often missing in more considered works. Unlike many books on the theory and practice of history, it contains numerous concrete examples of real historians and real history books to illustrate the more abstract argument it is propounding. In contrast to the majority of history primers and introductions to history of various kinds, it does not talk down to its readers but addresses them as equals. It is witty, amusing and entertaining even when it tackles the most recondite and intractable theoretical problems. It still retains after forty years its power to provoke. It tackles fundamental questions not just of history but also of politics and ethics. It deals with big topics and deals with them in a masterly fashion. Its range of reference, to historians, philosophers, writers and thinkers, is little short of astonishing. Carr knew a great deal and was a very clever man, and part of the seductive attraction of *What is History?* lies in the effortless display of learning and intelligence that it presents.

For the historian, *What is History?* is important for many reasons, not least for its insistence on the fact that, as Carr said, 'History is a process, and you cannot isolate a bit of process and study it on its own . . . everything is completely interconnected'.[70] Carr thought, rightly, that it was the job of historians to study whatever part of the past they chose to examine in the context of both what came before and after it, and the interconnections between their subject and its wider context. Above all, however, his book makes clear again and again that, whether we like it or not, there is always a subjective element in historical writing, for historians are individuals, people of their time, with views and assumptions about the world that they cannot eliminate from their writing and research, even if they can hope to restrain them, subordinate them to the intractabilities of the material with which they are working, and enable readers to study their work critically by making these views and assumptions explicit. It is in this respect that Carr has been most influential, and his views most widely accepted by historians; and for this reason more than any other that his work will endure.

## FURTHER READING

The Preface Carr wrote for the projected but never completed second edition of *What is History?* is printed together with an account of the notes he made in preparation for the new version, by R. W. Davies, in this edition of the book. Carr's *A History of Soviet Russia* was published in fourteen volumes from 1950 to 1978 by Macmillan – now Palgrave. There is a handy digest in his *The Russian Revolution from*

*Lenin to Stalin, 1917–1929,* published in 1979. The following year, Carr published a collection of some of his most important essays under the title *From Napoleon to Stalin.*

Carr's *Autobiography* is printed in Michael Cox (ed.) *E. H. Carr: A Reappraisal* (London, 2000), which also has a very perceptive critique of his views of history by Anders Stephanson, 'The Lessons of *What is History?*', pp. 283–303. Many of the other essays in the book are also very helpful in understanding Carr's life and work. Most important of all, however, is the biography by Jonathan Haslam, *The Vices of Integrity: E. H. Carr 1892–1982* (London, 1999), which contains an important chapter on the genesis and reception of *What is History?* and its relation to Carr's other work. Haslam's biography is the essential starting-point for anyone who is interested in Carr and his ideas. Carr's own papers are in the Special Collections section at Birmingham University Library and are briefly described in an Appendix to the volume of essays edited by Michael Cox.

There are many critiques of Carr's views on history. In his lifetime, the most cogent criticisms were made by his friend Isaiah Berlin, whose collected works are being edited for publication by Henry Hardy. See in particular his lecture/essay *Historical Inevitability* (London, 1954), reprinted in Isaiah Berlin, *The Proper Study of Mankind: An Anthology of Essays,* edited by Henry Hardy and Roger Housheer (London, 1997). The background to his views can be traced in the biography by Michael Ignatieff, *Isaiah Berlin: A Life* (London, 1998). From a more conservative angle, the most trenchant attack came from G. R. Elton, *The Practice of History* (2nd edition with an Afterword by Richard J. Evans, London, 2001). Arthur Marwick has also joined the chorus of criticism, both in his book *The Nature of History* (2nd edn, London, 2001) and in his article '"A Fetishism of Documents"? The Salience of Source-Based History', in H. Kozicki (ed.), *Developments in Modern Historiography* (New York, 1993) pp. 107–38.

*Introduction*

From the Althusserian Marxist angle there is Paul Hirst, *Marxism and Historical Writing* (London, 1985), while in the postmodernist corner there is Keith Jenkins, *On 'What is History?' From Carr and Elton to Rorty and White* (London, 1995), reviewed critically by Geoffrey Roberts, in *History and Theory* 36/2 (1997) pp. 249–60. Similar views are expressed by Alun Munslow in his discussion of *What is History?* on the website of London University's Institute of Historical Research, http://ihr.sas.ac.uk. The website also has a section devoted to the kind of questions raised by Carr.

More recent attempts to tackle these questions afresh have been made by Richard J. Evans, *In Defence of History* (2nd edn with a new Afterword, London, 2001), by C. Behan McCullagh, *The Truth of History* (London, 1998) and Robert F. Berkhofer, Jr, *Beyond the Great Story* (Cambridge, Mass., 1995). Carr's relativism is taken to new lengths in the engrossing and intelligently argued survey by Peter Novick, *That Noble Dream: The 'Objectivity Question' and the American Historical Profession* (Cambridge, Mass., 1988). Georg G. Iggers, *Historiography in the Twentieth Century* (Hanover, New Hampshire, 1997) is a level-headed and very readable account of the development of historical thought, mainly in Britain, France, Germany and the USA, during Carr's lifetime.

*Notes*

I am grateful to the University of Birmingham for granting me access to the Carr Papers in the special collections section of the University Library. I would like to thank Jonathan Haslam for his careful reading of a draft of this Introduction and his helpful suggestions. All views are my own.

1. E. H. Carr, 'An Autobiography' (1980) in Michael Cox (ed.), *E. H. Carr. A Critical Appraisal* (London, 2000), pp. xiii–xxii, here p. xiv.
2. 'E. H. Carr: Chronology of His Life and Work, 1892–1982', in ibid., pp. 339–43.
3. Carr, 'An Autobiography', pp. xv, xx.
4. Ibid., p. xiv.

5. E. H. Carr, 'Truth in History', *TLS*, 1 September 1950.

6. E. H. Carr, 'Progress in History', *TLS*, 18 July 1952.

7. E. H. Carr, 'Victorian History', *TLS*, 19 June 1953.

8. E. H. Carr, 'History without Bias', *TLS*, 30 December 1960.

9. Jonathan Haslam, *The Vices of Integrity. E. H. Carr 1892–1982* (London, 1999), pp. 192–6.

10. E. H. Carr, 'European Diplomatic History', *TLS*, 26 December 1954.

11. Michael Ignatieff, *Isaiah Berlin: A Life* (London, 1998) esp. Ch. 13.

12. E. H. Carr, *The Bolshevik Revolution*, Vol. I (London, 1950) pp. 5–6.

13. Haslam, *The Vices of Integrity*, p. 146.

14. Isaiah Berlin, reviewing *The Bolshevik Revolution* in the *Sunday Times*, 10 December 1950.

15. Ignatieff, *Isaiah Berlin*, pp. 205–6; Isaiah Berlin, *Historical Inevitability* (London, 1954) reprinted in Isaiah Berlin, *The Proper Study of Mankind: An Anthology of Essays*, edited by Henry Hardy and Roger Housheer (London, 1997) pp. 119–90, here p. 189; Haslam, *The Vices of Integrity*, pp. 197–8.

16. E. H. Carr, 'History and Morals', *TLS*, 17 December 1954.

17. Carr to Deutscher, 29 March 1960, cited in Haslam, *The Vices of Integrity*, p. 188.

18. Haslam, *The Vices of Integrity*, pp. 189–92.

19. Ved Mehta, *Fly and the Fly-Bottle. Encounters with British Intellectuals* (London, 1963) pp. 93–4.

20. Isaiah Berlin, letters column, *The Listener*, 18 May 1961.

21. E. H. Carr, letter, *The Listener*, 1 June 1961.

22. Isaiah Berlin, letter in *The Listener*, 15 June 1961.

23. Isaiah Berlin, *Karl Marx: His Life and Environment* (London, 1939); E. H. Carr, *Karl Marx: A Study in Fanaticism* (London, 1934).

24. Carr to Berlin, 27 June 1961, in University of Birmingham Library Special Collections, Box 11. All references to Carr's private correspondence in this Introduction are to documents in this file, unless otherwise noted.

25. Isaiah Berlin, letter in *The Listener*, 15 June 1961.

26. Berlin to Carr, 3 July 1961, and Carr to Berlin, 18 July 1961, both quoted in Haslam, *The Vices of Integrity*, p. 201.

27. Berlin, 'Mr Carr's Big Battalions', *New Statesman*, 5 January 1962, pp. 15–16.

28. 'Between Past and Future', *TLS*, 17 November 1961, pp. 813–14. For the indentification of Deutscher as the reviewer, see Haslam, *The Vices of Integrity*, pp. 204–5.

29. Carr to Isaac Deutscher, 17 December 1963.

30. E. H. Carr, *From Napoleon to Stalin* (London, 1980) pp. 262–3.

31. W. H. Walsh, in *English Historical Review*, July 1964 (clipping in Carr papers, Box 28); see also idem, *An Introduction to Philosophy of History* (3rd edn, London, 1967).

32. A. J. P. Taylor, 'Moving with the Times', *The Observer*, 22 October 1961.

33. Geoffrey Barraclough, 'Historical pessimism', *Guardian*, 20 October 1961.

34. *What is History?*, pp. 100–2.

35. John Carr, 'Foreword', Cox (ed.), *E. H. Carr*, p. ix.

36. Woodward to Carr, 9 May 1961.

37. *What is History?* p. 117.

38. J. D. Legge (Monash University), review clipping in Carr papers.

39. Isaiah Berlin, 'Mr Carr's Big Battalions'.

40. H. R. Trevor-Roper, 'E. H. Carr's Success Story', *Encounter*, May 1962, pp. 69–77, esp. pp. 75–6.

41. Mehta, *Fly and the Fly-Bottle*, p. 117.

42. April Carter, 'What is History?', in *Peace News*, 8 December 1961, p. 8.

43. Taylor, 'Moving with the Times'. The kulaks were allegedly wealthy peasants whose opposition to the collectivization of agriculture by Stalin in the early 1930s led to their mass deportation, imprisonment and execution by the Soviet regime.

44. Mehta, *Fly and the Fly-Bottle*, pp. 156–61.

45. A. J. P. Taylor, 'Moving with the Times'.

46. Mehta, *Fly and the Fly-Bottle*, p. 158.

47. 'Between Past and Future'.

48. Mehta, *Fly and the Fly-Bottle*, p. 158; Haslam, *The Vices of Integrity*, p. 211.

49. Haslam, *The Vices of Integrity*, pp. 194–6, citing Carr, 'Progress in History'.

50. Trevelyan to Carr, 15 December 1961.

51. Carr to Isaac Deutscher, 16 November 1965, quoted in Haslam, *The Vices of Integrity*, p. 207.

52. *What is History?* pp. 36–7 and 145–7.

53. Tim Mason, 'What of History?', *The New University* 8 (December, 1961), pp. 13–14.

54. G. R. Elton, *The Practice of History* (Sydney, 1967, reprinted London, 2001, with an Afterword by Richard J. Evans), pp. 170–1.

55. Ibid., pp. 176–81.

56. For details, see Evans, *In Defence of History* pp. 76–9.

57. 'Between Past and Future'; *What is History?* pp.20–1.

58. Carr to Postan, 3 December 1970.

59. E. H. Carr, *What is History?* (2nd edition, ed. R. W. Davies, esp. pp. lxxviii–lxxxiii; Carr papers, Box 11: Carr, typescript for an

article for the *TLS*, 11 June 1971 (urging English historians to study Marx).

60. Morton White, 'Searching for the Archimedean Point', *The New Leader*, 14 May 1962.

61. Carr to Moshe Lewin, 24 January 1967.

62. 'New Ways in History', *TLS* 7 April 1966, 28 July 1966, 8 September 1966. See also the criticisms of Carr from the *History Workshop* movement in Tim Mason to R. W. Davies, 20 February 1984.

63. For example, 'Between Past and Future'.

64. Alan Munslow, 'E. H. Carr (1892–1982) *What is History?*', *Reviews in History* (Institute of Historical Research, London, website).

65. Keith Jenkins, *On 'What is History?' From Carr and Elton to Rorty and White* (London, 1995) p. 61; reprised and in places copied word-for-word in Keith Jenkins, 'Rethinking *What is History?*', in Cox (ed.), *E. H. Carr*, pp. 304–22.

66. Anders Stephanson, 'The Lessons of *What is History?*', in Cox (ed.), *E. H. Carr*, pp. 283–303, here p. 300 n. 5.

67. See Richard J. Evans, *In Defence of History* (new edition with Afterword, London, 2001).

68. See Richard J. Evans, *Lying About Hitler: History, Holocaust and the David Irving Trial* (New York, 2001).

69. For the *reductio ad absurdum* of an approach to history based on moral judgments to the exclusion of any kind of interpretation or analysis, see Michael Burleigh, *The Third Reich: A New History* (London, 2001).

70. Mehta, *Fly and the Fly-Bottle*, pp. 159, 161.

## Introductory Note

E. H. CARR collected a great deal of material for the second edition of *What is History?*, but by the time of his death in November 1982 only the preface to this new edition had been written up.

The present posthumous edition begins with this preface, and a new chapter, 'From E. H. Carr's Files: Notes towards a Second Edition of *What is History?*', in which I have endeavoured to present some of the material and conclusions contained in Carr's large box of jottings, drafts and notes. These are followed by the unrevised text of the first edition.

Phrases placed in square brackets within quotations in the new chapter were inserted by myself. I am grateful to Catherine Merridale for carefully checking Carr's references, and to Jonathan Haslam and Tamara Deutscher for their comments. Carr's notes towards the second edition of *What is History?* are to be deposited with the E. H. Carr Papers in the Library of the University of Birmingham.

November 1984                                              R. W. Davies

## Preface to the Second Edition

WHEN in 1960 I completed the first draft of my six lectures, *What is History?*, the western world was still reeling from the blows of two world wars and two major revolutions, the Russian and the Chinese. The Victorian age of innocent self-confidence and automatic belief in progress lay far behind. The world was a disturbed, even menacing, place. Nevertheless signs had begun to accumulate that we were beginning to emerge from some of our troubles. The world economic crisis, widely predicted as a sequel to the war, had not occurred. We had quietly dissolved the British Empire, almost without noticing it. The crisis of Hungary and Suez had been surmounted, or lived down. De-Stalinization in the USSR, and de-McCarthyization in the USA, were making laudable progress. Germany and Japan had recovered rapidly from the total ruin of 1945, and were making spectacular economic advances. France under De Gaulle was renewing her strength. In the United States the Eisenhower blight was ending; the Kennedy era of hope was about to dawn. Black spots—South Africa, Ireland, Vietnam—could still be kept at arm's length. Stock exchanges round the world were booming.

These conditions provided, at any rate, a superficial justification for the expression of optimism and belief in the future with which I ended my lectures in 1961. The succeeding twenty years frustrated these hopes and this complacency. The cold war has been resumed with redoubled intensity, bringing with it the threat of nuclear extinction. The delayed economic crisis has set in with a vengeance, ravaging the industrial countries and spreading the cancer of unemployment throughout western society. Scarcely a country is now free from the antagonism of violence and terrorism. The revolt of the oil-producing states of the Middle East has brought a significant shift in power to the disadvantage of the western industrial nations. The 'third world' has been transformed from a passive into a positive and disturbing factor in world affairs. In these conditions any expression of optimism has come to seem absurd. The prophets of woe have everything on their side. The picture of impending doom, sedulously drawn by sensational writers and journalists and transmitted through the media, has penetrated the vocabulary of everyday speech. Not for centuries has the once popular prediction of the end of the world seemed so apposite.

Yet at this point commonsense prompts two important reservations. In the first place the diagnosis of hopelessness for the future, though it purports to be based on irrefutable facts, is an abstract theoretical construct. The vast majority of people simply do not believe in it; and this disbelief is made evident by their behaviour. People make love, conceive, bear and rear children with great devotion. Immense attention, private and public, is given to health and education in order to promote the well-being of the next generation. New sources of energy are constantly explored. New inventions increase the efficiency of production. Multitudes of 'small savers' invest in national savings bonds, in building societies and in unit trusts. Widespread enthusiasm is shown for the preservation of the national heritage, architectural and artistic, for the benefit of future generations. It is tempting to conclude that belief in early annihilation is confined to a group of disgruntled intellectuals who are responsible for the lion's share of current publicity.

1

My second reservation relates to the geographical sources of these predictions of universal disaster, which emanate predominantly—I should be tempted to say, exclusively—from western Europe and its overseas offshoots. This is not surprizing. For five centuries these countries had been the undisputed masters of the world. They could claim with some plausibility to represent the light of civilization in the midst of an outer world of barbarian darkness. An age which increasingly challenges and rejects this claim must surely build disaster. It is equally unsurprizing that the epicentre of the disturbance, the seat of the most profound intellectual pessimism, is to be found in Britain; for nowhere else is the contrast between nineteenth-century splendour and twentieth-century drabness, between nineteenth-century supremacy and twentieth-century inferiority, so marked and so painful. The mood has spread over western Europe and—perhaps to a lesser degree—north America. All these countries participated actively in the great expansionist era of the nineteenth century. But I have no reason to suspect that this mood prevails elsewhere in the world. The erection of insurmountable barriers to communication on one side, and the incessant flow of cold war propaganda on the other, render difficult any sensible assessment of the situation in the USSR. But one can scarcely believe that, in a country where a vast majority of the population must be aware that, whatever their current complaints, things are far better than they were twenty-five or fifty or a hundred years ago, widespread despair about the future has taken hold. In Asia both Japan and China in their different ways are in a forward-looking position. In the Middle East and Africa, even in areas which are at present in a state of turmoil, emergent nations are struggling towards a future in which, however blindly, they believe.

My conclusion is that the current wave of scepticism and

despair, which looks ahead to nothing but destruction and decay, and dismisses as absurd any belief in progress or any prospect of a further advance by the human race, is a form of élitism—the product of élite social groups whose security and whose privileges have been most conspicuously eroded by the crisis, and of élite countries whose once undisputed domination over the rest of the world has been shattered. Of this movement the main standard-bearers are the intellectuals, the purveyors of the ideas of the ruling social group which they serve ('The ideas of a society are the ideas of its ruling class'). It is irrelevant that some of the intellectuals in question may have belonged by origin to other social groups; for, in becoming intellectuals, they are automatically assimilated into the intellectual élite. Intellectuals by definition form an élite group.

What is, however, more important in the present context is that all groups in a society, however cohesive (and the historian is often justified in treating them as such), throw up a certain number of freaks or dissidents. This is particularly liable to happen among intellectuals. I do not refer to the routine arguments between intellectuals conducted on the basis of common acceptance of main presuppositions of the society, but of challenges to these presuppositions. In western democratic societies such challenges, so long as they are confined to a handful of dissidents, are tolerated, and those who present them can find readers and an audience. The cynic might say that they are tolerated because they are neither numerous nor influential enough to be dangerous. For more than forty years I have carried the label of an 'intellectual'; and in recent years I have increasingly come to see myself, and to be seen, as an intellectual dissident. An explanation is ready to hand. I must be one of the very few intellectuals still writing who grew up, not in the high noon, but in the afterglow of the great Victorian age of faith and optimism, and it is difficult for me even today to think in terms of a world in permanent and irretrievable decline. In the following pages I shall try to distance myself from prevailing trends among western intellectuals, and especially those of this country today, to show how and why I think they have gone astray and to strike out a claim, if not for an optimistic, at any rate for a saner and more balanced outlook on the future.

E. H. Carr

# From E. H. Carr's Files:
## Notes towards a Second Edition of
## What is History?

R. W. Davies

IN the last few years before his death in November 1982 Carr was preparing a substantially new edition of *What is History?* Undaunted by the setbacks to human progress which characterized the twenty years which had elapsed since the first edition in 1961, Carr proclaims in his Preface that the intention of the new work was 'to strike out a claim, if not for an optimistic, at any rate for a saner and more balanced outlook on the future.'

Only the preface was written up. But among Carr's papers a large box contains, together with an envelope crammed with reviews and correspondence relating to the 1961 edition, half-a-dozen brown foolscap folders bearing the titles: 'History–General; Causality–Determinism–Progress; Literature and Art; Theory of Revolution and Violence; Russian Revolution; Marxism and History; Future of Marxism'. He obviously intended to do much more work before completing the second edition. The folders contain the titles of many books and articles on which he had not yet made notes. But they also contain material which had already been partly processed: marked off-prints and articles torn from journals, and numerous handwritten jottings on bits of scrap paper of various sizes. Letters exchanged with Isaac Deutscher, Isaiah Berlin, Quentin Skinner and others about the philosophy and methodology of history are also included in the folders, obviously with the intention of drawing upon them for the new edition. Occasional typed or handwritten notes are obviously first drafts of sentences or paragraphs. No plan for the proposed new edition is available, but a jotting reads:

Disarray of History
Assaults of Statistics
Psychology

*Structuralism*
Disarray of Literature
Linguistics

*Utopia etc.*
[a further scrap of paper reads:
'*Last chapter*
Utopia
Meaning of History']

Carr evidently intended to write new sections or chapters dealing with topics neglected or inadequately covered in the first edition, as well as to expand the existing chapters of *What is History?* with responses to critics and with additional material illustrating and sometimes revising his argument. Sometimes an entirely new book on our present discontents and the world we should strive for seems to be struggling to emerge from his wide-ranging notes and jottings. Certainly he intended to provide a final chapter, or chapters, perhaps a completely rewritten version of Lecture VI on 'The Widening Horizon', which would present his own view on the meaning of history and his vision of the future, related more directly than any of his previous writings to current political concerns.

Carr evidently saw little reason to revise the argument of his first two lectures on the historian and his facts and the historian and society. As an example of the false claims of the empiricist approach to the historical facts, he cites Roskill, the eminent naval historian, who praised 'the modern school of historians' who 'regard their function as no more than to assemble and record the facts of their period with scrupulous accuracy and fairness'. For Carr such historians, if they really behaved as they claimed, would resemble the hero of a short story by the Argentine novelist Borges (translated as *Funes the Memorious*), who never forgot anything he had seen or heard or experienced but admitted that in consequence 'My memory is a garbage heap'. Funes was 'not very capable of thought' since 'to think is to forget differences, to generalize, to make abstractions.'[1] Carr defined and dismissed empiricism in history and the social sciences as the 'belief that all problems can be solved by the application of some scientific value-free method, i.e. that there is an objective right solution and way of reaching it—the supposed assumptions of science transferred to the social sciences'. Carr notes that Ranke, a talisman for empirical historians, was regarded by Lukacs as anti-historical in the sense that he presented a collection of events, societies and institutions, rather than a process of advance from one to another; 'history', wrote Lukacs, 'becomes a collection of exotic anecdotes'.[2]

Carr's notes provide weighty support for this onslaught on empiricism. Gibbon believed that the best history could only be written by an 'historian-philosopher', who distinguished those facts which dominate a system of relations:[3] he proclaimed his debt to Tacitus as 'the first of the historians who applied the science of philosophy to the study of facts'.[4] Vico distinguished *il certo* (what is factually correct) from *il vero*; *il certo*, the object of *coscienza*, was particular on the individual, *il vero*, the object of *scienza*, was common or general.[5] Carr attributed the 'thinness and lack of depth in so much recent English political and historical writing' to the difference in historical method which 'so fatally separated Marx from the thinkers of the English-speaking world':

The tradition of the English-speaking world is profoundly empirical. Facts speak for themselves. A particular issue is debated 'on its merits'. Themes, episodes, periods are isolated for historical study in the light of some undeclared, and probably unconscious, standard of relevance . . . . All this would have been anathema to Marx. Marx was no empiricist. To study the part without reference to the whole, the fact without reference to its significance, the event without reference to cause or consequence, the particular crisis without reference to the general situation, would have seemed to Marx a barren exercise.

The difference has its historical roots. Not for nothing has the English-speaking world remained so obstinately empirical. In a firmly established social order, whose credentials nobody wishes to question, empiricism serves to effect running repairs . . . . Of such a world nineteenth-century Britain provided the perfect model. But in a time when every foundation is challenged, and we flounder from crisis to crisis in the absence of any guide-lines, empiricism is not enough.[6]

In any case, the veil of so-called empiricism serves to conceal unconscious principles of selection. 'History,' Carr writes, 'is a particular conception of what constitutes human rationality: every historian, whether he knows it or not, has such a conception.' In *What is History?* Carr devoted much attention to the influence of the historical and social environment on the selection and interpretation of facts by the historian, an aspect of the human condition which had fascinated him since student days. His notes for the new edition further exemplify the relativity of historical knowledge. Herodotus found a moral justification for the dominance of Athens in the role she played in the Persian wars; and the Wars, demonstrating that the thinking

Greeks must widen their horizons, persuaded Herodotus to extend his enquiry to more peoples and places.[7] The Arab view of history was strongly influenced by sympathy for the nomadic way of life. The Arabs saw history as a continuous or cyclical process in which dwellers in towns or oases were overrun by desert nomads, who settled and were then in turn overrun themselves by fresh waves from the desert; for Arab historians, the settled life bred luxury which weakened civilized people in relation to the barbarians. In contrast Gibbon in eighteenth-century England saw history not as cyclical but as a triumphant advance: in his famous phrase 'every age has increased, and still increases, the real wealth, the happiness, the knowledge and perhaps the virtue of the human race'. And Gibbon saw history from the vantage point of a self-confident ruling class in a long-established settled civilization. He held that Europe was secure from the barbarians since 'before they can conquer they must cease to be barbarians'. Carr remarks that revolutionary eras exercise a revolutionary influence on the study of history: there is 'nothing like a revolution to create an interest in history'. The English historians of the eighteenth century emerged in the context of the triumph of the 'glorious revolution' of 1688. The French revolution undermined the 'a-historical outlook of the French enlightenment, which rested on a conception of unchangeable human nature'. In such times of rapid change the relativity of historical knowledge was widely recognized. Macaulay was merely stating the obvious to his contemporaries when he declared that 'the man who held exactly the same opinion about the Revolution in 1789, in 1794, in 1804, in 1814 and in 1834, would have been either a divinely inspired prophet or an obstinate fool'.[8]

Given the relativity of historical knowledge, in what sense can objective history be said to exist? In *What is History?* Carr argued that while no historian can claim for his own values an objectivity beyond history, an 'objective' historian can be said to be one 'with a capacity to rise above the limited vision of his own situation in society and in history', and with 'the capacity to project his vision into the future in such a way as to give him a more profound and more lasting insight into the past'. Several critics of *What is History?* strongly objected to this treatment of 'objectivity', and defended the traditional view that the objective historian is one who forms judgements on the basis of the evidence, despite his own preconceptions. Carr did not regard this as a serious criticism. His *History of Soviet Russia* often displays an extraordinary degree of 'objectivity' in the traditional sense, presenting evidence which other historians have frequently called upon to support interpretations which conflict with Carr's. But he regarded such conscientiousness as the necessary obligation of a competent historian; it did not mean that the historian's approach to the evidence was free from the influence of his social and cultural environment.

Nevertheless, Carr was prepared to acknowledge, somewhat cautiously, that progress occurs in the study of history as well as in the development of society, and that progress in historical knowledge is associated with increasing objectivity. In *What is History?* he acknowledged the great advances made by history in the past two centuries, and acclaimed the widening of our horizons from the history of élites to the history of the peoples of the whole world. Referring by way of example to the assessment of Bismarck's achievement by successive generations of historians, he argued (or admitted) 'that the historian of the 1920s was nearer to objective judgement than the historian of the 1880s, and that the historian of today is nearer than the historian of the 1920s'. But he then qualified this apparent acceptance of an absolute element in the historian's standard of objectivity, insisting that 'objectivity in history does not and cannot rest on some fixed and immovable standard of judgement existing here and now, but only on a standard which is laid up in the future and is evolved as the course of history advances.' The problem of objectivity in history evidently continued to trouble him after he had completed *What is History?* In his notes, while rejecting 'absolute and timeless objectivity' as 'an unreal abstraction', he writes: 'History requires the selection and ordering of facts about the past in the light of some principle or norm of objectivity accepted by the historian, which necessarily includes elements of interpretation. Without this, the past dissolves into a jumble of innumerable isolated and insignificant incidents, and history cannot be written at all.'

In *What is History?* Carr also approached the question of historical objectivity from another angle (though without using the term 'objectivity' in this context). He examined the resemblances and differences in method between history and the natural sciences. The resemblances proved to be greater than the differences. Natural scientists no longer see themselves as establishing universal laws by induction from observed facts, but as engaging in discoveries through the interaction of hypotheses and facts. And history, like the natural sciences, is concerned not as is sometimes supposed with unique events but with the interaction between the unique and the general. The historian is committed to generalization, and indeed 'the historian is not really interested in the unique, but in what is general in the unique'.

For the new edition Carr collected extensive notes on the methodology of science. The trend of his thought emerges in his jottings, and I reproduce a selection of them without attempting to impose my own version of Carr's unwritten argument upon them (I have numbered each separate jotting individually):

(1) Formal or logical criterion of scientific truth; Popper believed that 'genuine' science was distinguished by a timeless rational principle . . .

T. Kuhn rejected a single scientific method in favour of a succession of relativistic methods . . .

Transition from static to dynamic view of science, from form to function (or purpose).

Relativism (no single 'scientific method') drives Feyerabend, *Against Method* (1975) to total rejection of rationalism.[9]

(2) Plato, *Meno*, raised question of how it is possible to pursue an enquiry in ignorance of what we are looking for (para 80d).

'Not until we have for a long time unsystematically collected observations to serve as building materials, following the guidance of an idea concealed in our minds, and indeed only after we have spent much time in the technical disposition of these materials, do we first become capable of viewing the idea in a clearer light, and of outlining it architectonically as a whole.'

Kant, *Critique of Pure Reason* (1781), p. 835.

Popper's thesis that a hypothesis which fails to produce testable conclusions has no significance cannot be maintained (Natural Selection).

[See] M. Polanyi, *Encounter*, January 1972, from which the following [is also] taken . . .

Einstein in 1925 remarked to Heisenberg that 'Whether you can observe a thing or not depends on the theory which you use. It is the theory which decides what can be observed.'

(3) [Marked by Carr in a lecture by W. F. Weisskopf]

'We comprehend the formation of such [mountain] ranges by tectonic activities of the earth's crust, but we cannot explain why Mt. Blanc has the specific shape that we see today, nor can we predict which side of Mt. St. Helens will cave in at the next eruption . . .

'The occurrence of unpredictable events does not mean that the laws of nature are violated.'

(4) D. Struik, *Concise History of Mathematics* (1963) shows social rootedness of mathematics.

(5) The theory that the universe began in some random way with a big bang and is destined to dissolve into black holes is a reflexion of the cultural pessimism of the age. Randomness is an enthronement of ignorance.

(6) Belief in dominant importance of heredity was progressive so long as you believe that acquired characteristics were inherited.

When this was rejected, the belief in heredity became reactionary.

See argument in C. E. Rosenberg, *No Other Gods: On Science and American Social Thought* (1976) [especially p. 10].

From these jottings it is evident that Carr had come to the conclusion that the relativity of scientific knowledge was greater than he had previously suggested. Time and place exert great influence on the theory and practice of the natural scientist. The interplay between hypothesis and concrete material in natural science closely resembles the interplay between generalization and fact in history. Valid scientific hypotheses do not necessarily possess the capacity for precise prediction which is often attributed to them; in some natural sciences they closely resemble the generalizations of the historian.

In the Lecture on 'Causation in History' in *What is*

*History?* Carr examined the nature of historical generalization more closely. The historian is confronted with a multiplicity of causes of an historical event, and seeks to establish 'some hierarchy of courses which would fix their relation to each other'. In his notes for the new edition, Carr reproduces passages from Montesquieu and Tocqueville which adopt a similar point of view. Causes, wrote Montesquieu, 'become less arbitrary as they have a more general effect. Thus we know better what gives a certain character to a nation than what gives a particular mentality to an individual . . . what forms the spirit of societies that have embraced a way of life than what forms the character of a single person.'[10] And on Tocqueville's distinction between 'ancient and general causes' and 'particular and recent causes'[11] Carr commented: 'This is sensible; general equals long-term; the historian is primarily interested in the long-term'.

For the practising historian the attempt to explain historical events in terms of long-term, general or significant causes immediately gives rise to the problem of the role of accident in history. In *What is History?* Carr acknowledged that accidents can modify the course of history, but argued that they should not enter into the historian's hierarchy of significant causes. The accident of Lenin's premature death played a role in the history of the Soviet Union in the 1920s, but was not a 'real' cause of what happened in the sense that it was a rational and historically significant explanation which could be applied to other historical situations. Developing this idea further after the publication of *What is History?* he wrote in his notes that 'history is in fact subject to sufficient regularities to make it a serious study, though these regularities are from time to time upset by extraneous events.'

The problem of accident proved particularly troublesome in that special case of accident, the role of the individual in history. Carr returned again and again to this issue, which of course loomed large in his own study of the development of the Soviet Union in the years of Stalin's rise to power. His file 'Individual in History' places the problem in a broad historical context. He suggests that the cult of the individual is 'an élitist doctrine', because 'individualism can only mean setting the individual agent against the background of an impersonal mass'. An extreme insistence on the absolute rights of the free individual has found widespread support among intellectuals. Aldous Huxley, the foremost British proponent of this view in the 1920s and 1930s, claimed in his aptly-titled *Do As You Will* that 'The purpose of life . . . is the purpose we put into it. Its meaning is whatever we may choose to call its meaning . . . . Every man has an inalienable right to the major premiss of his philosophy of life.'[12] In the 1930s, Sartre's influential *Being and Nothingness* distinguished between the being 'for-itself'—pure consciousness of the individual, absolute freedom and responsibility—and the being 'in-itself', the material, objective, non-conscious world. At this stage he was anti-Marxist, with 'traits of anarchism (never absent in Sartre)'. And in 1960, although *Critique of Dialectical Reason* purported to recognize Marxism as the 'ultimate philosophy of our age', in fact, according to Carr, 'his brand of existentialism, total freedom, individuality and subjectivity was incompatible with Marxism'. Similarly Adorno, while influenced by Marxism, 'wanted to rescue the individual from complete submission in a world of technocracy and bureaucracy, and also in a world of closed systems of philosophy (Hegel's idealism, Marx's materialism)'. And for Freud the freedom of the individual was not the product of civilization; on the contrary, the effect of civilization was to restrict the individual.[13]

The claim that the individual was fettered by society and

should be freed from these fetters is partly cognate with, partly in conflict with, the equally long-established claim that some individuals are actually able to act unfettered by society, which frequently appears in the form of an insistence on the overwhelming importance of Great Men in History. Andrew Marvell emphatically claimed such a role for Cromwell:

> 'Tis he the force of scattered time contracts
> And in one year the work of ages acts.

In contrast Samuel Johnson declared:

> How small of all that human hearts endure
> That part that kings or laws can cause or cure.

But Johnson's was a mere 'rearguard action', writes Carr, 'against the belief that kings and laws do cause and cure evils'.

Against those who claim a decisive role for the individual will, which is independent or autonomous from society, Marx argued that the view which 'takes the *isolated* man as its starting point' is 'absurd' (*abgeschmackt*). Man 'originally appears as a generic being, a herd animal', who 'individualizes himself through the process of history'; 'exchange itself is a major agent of this individualization'.[14] Macaulay, writing about Milton, observed that 'in proportion as men know more, and think more, they look less at individuals and more at classes'.[15] And Tocqueville in 1852 gave classic expression to the notion that the actions of individual politicians are determined by forces outside themselves:

> Among all civilized peoples the political sciences create, or at least give shape to, general ideas; and from

these general ideas are formed the problems in the midst of which politicians must struggle, and also the laws which they imagine they create. The political sciences form a sort of intellectual atmosphere breathed by both governors and governed in society, and both unwittingly derive from it the principles of their action.

Tolstoy consistently gave extreme expression to the view that individuals play an insignificant role in history: in one of the drafts of the epilogue to *War and Peace*, he bluntly stated that 'historical personages are the products of their time, emerging from the connection between contemporary and preceding events'.[16] His view was already fully formed by 1867:

> The zemstvo [Russian local government], the courts, war or the absence of war etc. are all manifestations of the social organism—the swarm organism (as with bees): anyone can manifest it, and in fact the best are those who don't know themselves what they are doing and why—and the result of their common labour is always a uniform activity and one that is familiar to the laws of zoology. The zoological activity of the soldier, the emperor, the marshal of the gentry or the ploughman is the lowest form of activity, an activity in which—the materialists are right—there is no arbitrariness.[17]

And thirty years later, on the outbreak of the Boer War, he wrote that it was no good being angry with 'the Chamberlains and the Wilhelms'; 'all history is a series of just such acts by all politicians', resulting from the effort to support the exceptional wealth of the few with new markets 'while the masses of the people are ground down by hard work'.[18]

Carr broadly shared the approach of Marx and Tocqueville. He noted that 'Individuals in History have "roles"; in some sense the role is more important than the individual'. He observed of Ramsay Macdonald that his 'wobbling was the result not so much of his personal character (significant only in so far as it fitted him for the leadership) as of the basic dilemma of the whole group represented by the Labour Party'. More generally he claimed to be concerned not so much to assess individual politicians as 'to analyse the group interests and attitudes which mould their thinking'. The way individual minds work, he wrote, 'isn't all that important for a historian', and it is better to 'look at history rather less in terms of conscious personal behaviour, and more in terms of subconscious group situations and attitudes.' In this spirit he noted wryly that a book about Hitler 'begins by attributing everything to Hitler's personality, and ends by talking of the instability and incapacity of the Weimar regime.'[19]

But Carr did not hold to Tolstoy's extreme position: his travails as a working historian constantly drove him back to 'Cleopatra's nose'. Remarking that the problem of accident in history 'still interests and puzzles me', he again insisted in his notes, as he had in *What is History?*, that while Lenin's death was due to causes extraneous to history, it affected its course. He went on to add that 'even if you maintain that in the long run everything would have turned out much the same, there is a short run which is important, and makes a great deal of difference to a great many people.' There is here a marked shift in emphasis as compared with his discussion of historical accident in *What is History?* This was a prelude to his striking comments on the role of Lenin and Stalin in his interview with Perry Anderson on the occasion of the completion of his *History*. He insisted that 'Lenin, if he had lived through the twenties and thirties in the full possession of his faculties, would have faced exactly the same problems', and would have embarked on the creation of large-scale mechanized agriculture, on rapid industrialization, on the control of the market, and on the control and direction of labour. But he would have been able 'to minimize and mitigate the element of coercion':

> Under Lenin the passage might not have been altogether smooth, but it would have been nothing like what happened. Lenin would not have tolerated the falsification of the record in which Stalin constantly indulged . . . . The USSR under Lenin would never have become, in Ciliga's phrase, 'the land of the big lie'. These are my speculations.[20]

Carr here attributes a substantial role to accident in a crucial period of Soviet history. This was an oral statement, rather than a carefully considered judgement. But in the more temperate language of his *History*, he also wrote that 'Stalin's personality, combined with the primitive and cruel traditions of Russian bureaucracy, imparted to the revolution from above a particularly brutal quality'.[21] The 'revolution from above' was broadly determined by the long-term causes which must be the prime consideration of the historian, but the extent of the coercion used was an accident of history.

In various notes and letters in his files, Carr assesses the present state of historical studies. He points to Marxist influences as a major new trend of the past sixty years:

> Since the first world war the impact of the materialist conception of history on historical writings has been very strong. Indeed, one might say that all serious historical work done in this period has been moulded by its influence. The symptom of this change has been the

replacement, in general esteem, of battles, diplomatic manoeuvres, constitutional arguments and political intrigues as the main topics of history—'political history' in the broad sense—by the study of economic factors, of social conditions, of statistics of population, of the rise and fall of classes. The increasing popularity of sociology has been another feature of the same development; the attempt has sometimes been made to treat history as a branch of sociology.

In *What is History?* Carr had already noted the positive influence of sociology on history, remarking that 'the more sociological history becomes, and the more historical sociology becomes, the better for both'. In his notes for the new edition, he declared more strongly: 'Social history is the bedrock. To study the bedrock alone is not enough; and becomes tedious; perhaps this is what has happened to Annales. But you can't dispense with it.'

While recognising these positive developments, Carr insists that in terms of the general or prevailing trends both history and the social sciences are in crisis. Carr notes the shallow empiricism of 'the flight from history into sectoral specialization' (which he castigates as 'a form of self-mutilation'), and the tendency of historians to take cover in methodology (he remarks that the 'cult of "quantitative" history, which makes statistical information the source of all historical enquiry, perhaps carries the materialist conception of history to the point of absurdity'). And this crisis within history itself has been accompanied by the flight from history into the social sciences, which Carr also regards as a conservative or even reactionary trend:

> History is preoccupied with fundamental processes of change. If you are allergic to these processes, you abandon history and take cover in the social sciences.

Today anthropology, sociology, etc. flourish. History is sick. But then our society too is sick.

He also points out that 'of course, "taking cover" also goes on within the social sciences—economists in econometrics, philosophers in logic and linguistics, literary critics in the analysis of stylistic techniques'. Talcott Parsons provides an obvious example of a sociologist who 'carried abstraction so far that he lost all touch with history'.

Carr devotes much attention to structuralism (or 'structural functionalism'). He once remarked in conversation that structuralists at least had the merit of treating the past as a whole, avoiding the pitfalls of over-specialization. But he believed that on the whole structuralism had exercised a harmful influence on the study of history. He compares the structural or 'horizontal' approach 'which analyses a society in terms of the functional or structural inter-relation of its parts or aspects', and the historical or 'vertical' approach, 'which analyses it in terms of where it has come from and where it is going to'. He suggests that 'every sensible historian will agree that both approaches are necessary' (a blunter note scribbled on a scrap of paper remarks that 'the distinction between narrative history and structural history is bogus'):

But it makes a lot of difference which attracts [the historian's] main emphasis and concern. This depends partly, no doubt, on his temperament, but largely on the environment in which he works. We live in a society which thinks of change chiefly as change for the worse, dreads it and prefers the 'horizontal' view which calls only for minor adjustments.

Elsewhere Carr remarks that 'the former approach is conservative in the sense that it examines a static condition, and the latter radical in the sense that it turns on change':

> However much LS [Levi-Strauss] may quote Marx for his purpose . . . I suspect that structuralism is the fashionable philosophy of a conservative period.

Carr's notes include several items on Levi-Strauss, notably an interview in *Le Monde*, the heading of which seems to confirm Carr's worst suspicions: '*L'idéologie marxiste, communiste et totalitaire n'est qu'une ruse de l'histoire*'.[22]

Carr's far-reaching criticism, and on the whole negative evaluation, of the present state of historical studies is accompanied by a positive assertion of the importance of the discipline of history in its own right. He proclaims the need for 'general history', which brings together legal, military, demographic, cultural and other branches of history and examines the interconnections between them. Equally he insists that history is not the mere handmaiden of the social sciences, going to them for its theory and supplying them with materials:

> I recognise that many present-day historians are dead because they have no theory. But the theory which they lack is a theory of history, not one delivered from outside. What is needed is a two-way traffic . . . . The historian must learn from the economic, demographic, military etc. etc. specialists. But the economist, demographer, etc. etc. will also die unless he works within a broader historical pattern which only the 'general' historian can provide. The trouble is . . . that historical theories are by nature theories of change, and that we live in a society which wants or reluctantly accepts only subsidiary or 'specialized' changes in a stabilized historical equilibrium.

But Carr of course believed that the outlook of the

historian depended on his social environment; and in Britain of the 1970s he could not expect that his advice would be welcomed by more than a minority of radical or dissident historians:

> To a society which is full of confusion about the present, and has lost faith in the future, the history of the past will seem a meaningless jumble of unrelated events. If our society regains its mastery of the present, and its vision of the future, it will also, in virtue of the same process, renew its insight into the past.

This passage was written in 1974, several years before the upsurge in Britain of conservative doctrines and of a new confidence in a conservative future. Since then, and since Carr's death, an alternative has emerged to the lack of faith in the future and the accompanying empiricism which were previously the prevailing orthodoxy among British historians. Remarkable efforts have been make by conservative politicians and historians to encourage confidence in the future by restoring patriotic British history to the centre of the historical curriculum. Sir Keith Joseph, Minister of Education, supported by Lord Hugh Thomas, has called for schools to pay much more attention to British history, and less to world history. Professor G. R. Elton in his inaugural lecture as Regius Professor of Modern History condemned the harmful influences of the social sciences on undergraduate history teaching in Cambridge, and insisted that the study of English history should occupy a dominant position in the history tripos. English history would show 'the manner in which this society managed to civilize power and order itself through constant changes'; 'an age of uncertainty, beset by false faiths and the prophets of constant innovation, badly needs to know its roots.'[23] These events would have seemed to

Carr symptomatic of a sick society which sought comfort in recollection of a glorious past, and to provide a striking demonstration of the extent to which historians reflect the prevailing trends in society.

Carr intended that the new edition of *What is History?* would consider the crisis of historical studies in the broad context of the social and intellectual crisis of our times. To this end he assembled a file on Literature and Art, which were not discussed as separate topics in his original lectures. This file includes notes both on literature itself and on literary and artistic criticism. The work is in a very preliminary stage. The thread of his argument is that literature and literary criticism, like history and the natural and social sciences, are influenced or moulded by the social environment. Two contrasting quotations leap to the eye in his ˙notes. While Orwell declared that 'All art is propaganda'[24] Marx, who himself left many notes on the influence of society on the arts, nevertheless warned in the *Introduction to the Critique of Political Economy* that 'as regards art, it is well known that some of its peaks by no means correspond to the general development of society; nor do they therefore to the material structure, the skeleton as it were of its organisation'.[25]

On Carr's assessment, Marx's reservations did not apply to the twentieth century, which was primarily characterized by pessimism, inaction and hopelessness. For Carr, Hardy was 'the novelist of a world that makes no sense, that is fundamentally awry, not that has gone wrong, or can be put right, but a world of timeless wrongness and senselessness—hence an absolute pessimism.' A. E. Housman remarked that 'I have seldom written poetry unless I was rather out of health',[26] and T. S. Eliot commented sympathetically 'I believe that I understand that sentence'. 'Both wrote "sick" poetry', Carr comments sharply, 'Neither is a rebel.' A series of quotations in Carr's notes illustrate Eliot's lack of hope and pessimism. While Shakespeare's Sonnet No. 98 was a celebration of April, Eliot's *The Waste Land* sees April as the cruellest month. In *Gerontion*, written in 1920, Eliot complained that history 'deceives with whispering ambitions, Guides us by vanities'.[27] *The Waste Land* treats crowds of workers crossing London Bridge as dead people, while Wyndham Lewis writes of 'half-dead people' whose extermination would not matter.[28] In his testament Kafka, the prophet of failure, significantly ordered the destruction of his writings; our world, Kafka once said, is one of God's 'bad moods'; outside our world there was 'plenty of hope—for God . . . only not for us'.[29] And even Orwell, according to Carr, 'ends up in the same position as Eliot, despair about the human race, especially in form of dislike of lower classes—a form of élitism'. Two modern classics with a significant coincidence of title, Cavafy's poem 'Waiting for the Barbarians' and Beckett's 'Waiting for Godot', both present 'helpless expectant inaction'. And the cult of Hermann Hesse celebrates a writer whom Carr described as 'a solipsist refugee from a world in which he had ceased to believe'.

A further group of notes seeks to place twentieth-century literary criticism in its social context. F. R. Leavis 'revived Matthew Arnold's vision of a class of disinterested intellectuals constituting the flower of a society and standing above it'. The new literary criticism 'began with I. A. Richards, who distinguished between objective (scientific) and subjective (emotive) elements in literature'; his successors 'tried to equate the literary critic with scientific observers, applying objective criteria to the text and ignoring all questions of derivation or context'. On these developments Carr comments:

The formalists of the 1930s, 1940s and 1950s, and the structuralists of the 1960s and 1970s sought to isolate literature as a 'pure' entity confined within the limits of language, and uncontaminated by any other reality.

But literary criticism cannot be rooted exclusively in literature, since the critic himself is outside literature and brings with him elements from other spheres.

And as for 'linguistic philosophy' (a misnomer, as it is an escape from philosophy as traditionally conceived), like 'art for art's sake', it has no commitment to any idea.[30] It has no application to ethics or politics, and pays no attention to history: 'even the idea that words change their meaning was absent'.

In the last chapters of Carr's new edition he intended, in opposition to the prevailing pessimism of recent years, to reassert that man's past had by and large been a story of progress and to proclaim his confidence in man's future. In *What is History?* he noted that the view of history as progress, instituted by the rationalists of the Enlightenment, had achieved its greatest influence when British self-confidence and power were at their height. In the twentieth century, however, the crisis of western civilization had led many historians and other intellectuals to reject the hypothesis of progress. In his notes for the new edition, he distinguishes three aspects of the Age of Progress: the Expansion of the World, which began in 1490; Economic Growth, starting perhaps in the sixteenth century; and the Expansion of Knowledge, from 1600 onwards. The Elizabethan period, conscious of the expansion of the world, was the first brilliant phase of the Age of Progress. Macaulay, the greatest Whig historian, depicted history as a triumphant progress culminating in the Reform Bill.[31] It is clear from Carr's notes that he intended to provide further evidence in the new edition of *What is History?*, from medicine and other fields, that progress has fundamentally depended upon and resulted from the transmission of acquired skills from one generation to another.

Since the first world war belief in history as progress has become increasingly unfashionable. Descent into the depths of despair has sometimes been a trifle premature: 'Karl Kraus celebrated the collapse of the Austro-Hungarian Empire with a dramatic extravaganza called *The Last Days of Mankind.*' But scepticism about progress in the past and pessimism about prospects for the future have become more powerful and more assertive as the twentieth century has moved on. Popper, who gave a lecture a quarter of a century ago entitled 'The History of our Times: An Optimist's View', in 1979 gave a further lecture in which he remarked 'It so happens that I do not believe in progress.'[32] To some historians, the idea of progress is an outmoded joke: Richard Cobb wrote of Lefèbvre that 'he was a very naive man, who believed in human progress'.[33]

Carr believed in human progress in the past, and that 'an understanding of the past . . . carries with it an enhanced insight into the future.' He thus agreed with Hobbes that 'of our conceptions of the past we make a future'.[34] But he added the important comment that 'the converse would be almost equally true': our vision of the future influences our insight into the past. There was force in the aphorism with which Ernst Bloch concluded *Das Prinzip Hoffnung*: '*the true genesis is not in the beginning but in the end.*'[35]

In a time of doubt and despair Carr considered that it was particularly important for him as a historian to examine and set out his own understanding of the present and vision of the future. Over forty years previously he had argued that Utopia and reality were two essential facets of political science, and that 'sound political thought and sound political life will be found only where both have their place.'[36] In the intervening years he had acquired a reputation as an austere realist. But in the brief autobiographical memoir which he prepared a few year or so before his death, he commented: 'Perhaps the world is divided between cynics, who find no sense in anything, and Utopians who make sense of things on the basis of some magnificent unverifiable assumption about the future. I prefer the latter.' A jotting in Carr's files headed 'Hope' comments: 'Function of Utopia is to make the day-dream concrete . . . Utopia will reconcile the individual with the universal interest. True Utopia distinguished from idle (unmotivated) optimism.'

In Carr's view the two great students of classical British capitalism, Adam Smith and Karl Marx, each combined a profound insight into society with an underlying Utopia:

A. Smith, who wrote a *Theory of Modern Sentiments*, in the *Wealth of Nations* isolated the propensity 'to truck barter and exchange' as the main driving force of human action.

This was an insight of genius, not into human nature as such, but into the character of the society which was about to develop in western Europe (and in USA); and as such it promoted that development.

The same is true of Marx's insight that capitalism would collapse under the weight of the worker's refusal to tolerate the degree of exploitation involved.

But Smith's Utopia of the world of the invisible hand, and Marx's dictatorship of the proletariat, developed seamy sides as soon as the attempt was made to realize them in practice.

As early as 1933 Carr had referred to Marx as having 'a claim to be regarded as the most far-seeing genius of the nineteenth century and one of the most successful prophets in history.'[37] His files on 'Marxism and History' and 'Marxism and the Future' contain many notes from Marx,

Engels, Lenin and their leading followers, from which it is evident that he intended to base his own assessment of present and future on a careful appraisal of Marx and Marxism. In several of his recent writings he made it clear that, like his friend Herbert Marcuse, he believed that 'in the West today, the proletariat—meaning, as Marx meant by the term, the organized workers in industry—is not a revolutionary, perhaps even a counter-revolutionary force.'[38] He noted that scepticism about the incapacity of the proletariat to govern had resulted in 'Trotsky's ultimate relapse into pessimism',[39] and that a negative assessment of the proletariat underlay the pessimism of Marcuse:

> *Reason and Revolution.* The power of negation is embodied in the proletariat.
>    Interested in liberation of the individual personality from repressive society—Freud.
>    [In Marcuse's] *Eros and Civilization*—doubt about ability of proletariat to produce a non-repressive society.
>
> *Soviet Marxism.* Soviet history demonstrated failure of Russian proletariat to produce non-repressive society—failure due to failure of proletariat in advanced countries.
>
> *One-Dimensional Man* shows that proletariat has been engulfed in industrial society so that society becomes in principle unchangeable.
>    Result is total pessimism—divorce of Left theory from reality: 'There is no ground on which theory and practice, thought and action meet'.[40]

Carr on the whole accepted such criticisms of Marx, but he drew no such pessimistic conclusions. In his autobiographical memoir he declared:

I cannot indeed foresee for western society in anything like its present form any prospect but decline and decay, perhaps but not necessarily ending in dramatic collapse. But I believe that new forces and movements, whose shape we cannot yet guess, are germinating beneath the surface, here or elsewhere. That is my unverifiable Utopia . . . I suppose I should call it 'socialist', and am to this extent Marxist. But Marx did not define the content of socialism except in a few Utopian phrases; and nor can I.

How then did Carr himself assess the development and decay of the capitalist system; what 'new forces and movements' had he detected? Part of his answer was given in a rough draft in his notes headed 'Marxism and History', which appears to have been written in about 1970. While this was incomplete, and would certainly have been considerably revised before publication, it conveys well the spirit of Carr's view of the present and future:

The shape of the world has, therefore, changed out of recognition in the past fifty years. The former colonies of the western European Powers—India, Africa, Indonesia—have asserted their full independence. Of the Latin American countries only Mexico and Cuba have taken the path of revolution; but elsewhere economic development points the way to more complete independence. The most spectacular event of this period has been the rise of the USSR—the former Russian Empire—and more recently of China to positions of world power and world importance. The sense of uncertainty .created by these changes, whose consequences still lie in the future, contrasts sharply with the relative stability and security of the nineteenth-century world pattern. It is out of this atmosphere of uncertainty and insecurity that current visions of the new society are born.

It is a fact of the highest significance that the Russian revolution—and, after it, the Chinese and Cuban revolutions—professedly based themselves on the teaching of Karl Marx. Marx was the most powerful prophet of the decline and fall of the nineteenth-century capitalist system, still in its heyday in the period when he wrote. It is natural that those who sought to challenge this system, and rejoice in its downfall, should have appealed to the authority of Marx. It is also natural that visions of a new society to replace nineteenth-century capitalism should draw inspiration from Marxism. These visions are necessarily in part Utopian; Marx's writings on the future society were scanty and often Utopian in character. Some of his predictions have been frustrated or have proved unworkable, and this has already led to controversy and confusion among his followers. But the power of his analysis is undeniable; and any picture that can be drawn, however speculatively, of a future society must contain a large infusion of Marxist conceptions.

Marx was the prophet of productivity, of industrialization as the path to the highest forms of productivity, of modernization through the use of the most developed forms of technology. His writings, from the *Communist Manifesto* onwards, are full of eulogies of the achievements of capitalism, which liberated the processes of production from feudalist fetters, and set in motion throughout the world a modern technically developed, expansive economy. But Marx believed himself to have demonstrated by his analysis that bourgeois capitalism, based on the principles of individual private enterprise, was forging through its very success new fetters which would bring to a standstill the further expansion of production, which would take the control of production out of the hands of the bourgeois capitalist and substitute some form of social control by the workers themselves. Only thus could the expansion of productivity be maintained and intensified. One of the few pictures offered by Marx of a future communist society was that there 'the springs of wealth will flow more abundantly'.

In a world where large masses of people still do not enjoy even the most elementary material benefits of modern civilization, it is not surprising that these doctrines should have powerfully influenced the popular vision of a new society. Nor is it surprising (though it is the opposite of what Marx expected) that these doctrines should have made their most convincing appeal, not in advanced countries, whose peoples enjoyed in the past the great achievements of bourgeois capitalism, and find it difficult to believe that the potentialities of this system are even yet exhausted, but in the backward countries where bourgeois capitalism had appeared, either not at all, or as an alien and mainly oppressive force. The Russian revolution occurred in a technically backward country, where the bourgeois capitalist transformation of the economy and of society had scarcely begun; its first function, as Lenin said, was 'to complete the bourgeois revolution' before it could pass on to the socialist revolution. Since the second world war, the revolution has spread to countries where a bourgeois revolution had not even begun. The vision of a future society which, stepping over the now obsolete bourgeois capitalist revolution, will achieve the industrialization and modernization of the economy, and the higher productivity which goes with it, through some form of social and planned control of production, dominates today the whole world that lies outside the sphere of the western European nations.

Carr went on to add that 'the political aspects of this vision remain, however, blurred and elusive. Marxism gives little help. The conception of a society controlled by the workers proved to have little relevance in Russia, where the proletariat was small; it has no relevance at all in less advanced countries where a proletariat does not exist.' Nevertheless, revolution in these countries was likely to bring the capitalist system to an end, and provide the possibility of achieving Carr's 'unverifiable Utopia':

I think we have to consider seriously the hypothesis [he declared in September 1978] that the world revolution of which [the Bolshevik revolution] was the first stage, and which will complete the downfall of capitalism, will prove to be the revolt of the colonial peoples against capitalism in the guise of imperialism.[41]

*Notes*

1. J. L. Borges, *A Personal Anthology* (1972) pp. 32–3.
2. G. Lukacs, *The Historical Novel* (1962) pp. 176, 182.
3. Edward Gibbon, *Essai sur l'étude de la litterature* (1761).
4. Gibbon, *Decline and Fall of the Roman Empire*, Bury (ed.), (1909) ch. 9, p. 230.
5. G. Vico, *Principj di scienza nuovo* (1744) Books I, IX and X, translated as *New Science of G. Vico* (1968), paras. 137, 321.
6. This passage, in typescript in his notes, appears in Carr's essay on Lukacs in *From Napoleon to Stalin* (1980) p. 250.
7. *The Greek Historians*, M. I. Finley (ed.), (1959) Introduction, pp. 4, 6.
8. G. Macaulay, *Works* (1898) viii, 431 (from an essay on Sir James Mackintosh).
9. P. Feyerabend, *Against Method: Outline of an Anarchistic Theory of Knowledge* (1975), concludes, from the 'rich material provided by history', that only one principle can be defended for all circumstances and times: 'anything goes' (p. 27).
10. 'An Essay on Causes affecting Minds and Characters', in Montesquieu, *The Spirit of Laws*, ed. D. W. Carruthers (1977) p. 417.
11. See A. de Tocqueville, *De l'ancien regime* (trans. S. Gilbert, 1966), II, III, especially p. 160.
12. A. Huxley, *Do As You Will* (1929), p. 101.

13. S. Freud, *Civilization and its Discontents* (1975) p. 32; another of Carr's jottings observed that 'Freud's unconscious is individual; nothing to do with Jung's "collective unconsciousness".'

14. *Grundrisse* (Berlin, 1953) pp. 395–6.

15. *Works* (1898) vii, 6.

16. L. Tolstoi, *Polnoe sobranie sochinenii*, xv (1955) 279.

17. Letter to Samarin, 10 January 1867, in *Tolstoy's Letters*, R. F. Christian (ed.), i (1978) 211.

18. Letter to Volkonsky, 4/16 December 1899, ibid., ii, 585.

19. This was a reference to Sebastian Haffner, *The Meaning of Hitler* (1979).

20. *From Napoleon to Stalin* (1980) pp. 262–3 (interview with Perry Anderson, September 1978).

21. *A History of Soviet Russia* (1978) xi, 448.

22. *Le Monde*, 21–22 January 1979.

23. G. R. Elton, *The History of England: Inaugural Lecture delivered 26 January 1984* (Cambridge, 1984) especially pp. 9–11, 26–9; see also his attack on family history in *New York Review of Books*, 14 June 1984.

24. G. Orwell, *Collected Essays, Journalism and Letters* (1968) i, 448 (originally appeared in *Inside the Whale* (1940)).

25. Translated in K. Marx, *The German Ideology*, C. J. Arthur (ed.), (1970) p. 149.

26. A. E. Housman, *The Name and Nature of Poetry* (1933) p. 49.

27. T. S. Eliot, *Collected Poems 1909–1962* (1963) p. 40.

28. D. B. Wyndham Lewis, *Blasting and Bombardiering* (1937) p. 115.

29. Max Brod, *Kafka: a Biography* (1947) p. 61.

30. See J. Sturrock, *Structuralism and Since* (1979).

31. *Works* (1898) xi, 456–8 and cf. 489–91; but Carr also asks 'Is Macaulay's vision of the New Zealander (*Essay on Ranke's History of the Popes*) incompatible with belief in progress?'; Macaulay imagined a New Zealander of the future standing on a broken arm of London Bridge to sketch the ruin of St. Paul's, but in the same paragraph referred to the future greatness of the New World (Macaulay's *Essays*, selected and introduced by H. Trevor-Roper (1965) p. 276).

32. *Encounter*, November 1979, p. 11; in this lecture Popper nevertheless still claimed to be an optimist.

33. *A Second Identity* (1969) p. 100.

34. Thomas Hobbes on Human Nature, *Works* (1840) iv, 16.

35. Ernst Bloch, *Das Prinzip Hoffnung* (1956) iii, 489.

36. *The Twenty Years' Crisis, 1919–1939* (1939).

37. *Fortnightly Review*, March 1933, p. 319.

38. *From Napoleon to Stalin* (1980) p. 271.

39. See Knei-Paz, *The Social and Political Thought of Leon Trotsky* (1978) p. 423.

40. H. Marcuse, *One Dimensional Man* (1968) pp. 11–12.

41. *From Napoleon to Stalin* (1980) p. 275.

I

# The Historian and His Facts

WHAT is history? Lest anyone think the question meaningless or superfluous, I will take as my text two passages relating respectively to the first and second incarnations of the *Cambridge Modern History*. Here is Acton in his report of October 1896 to the Syndics of the Cambridge University Press on the work which he had undertaken to edit:

> It is a unique opportunity of recording, in the way most useful to the greatest number, the fullness of the knowledge which the nineteenth century is about to bequeath. . . . By the judicious division of labour we should be able to do it, and to bring home to every man the last document, and the ripest conclusions of international research.
>
> Ultimate history we cannot have in this generation; but we can dispose of conventional history, and show the point we have reached on the road from one to the other, now that all information is within reach, and every problem has become capable of solution.[1]

And almost exactly sixty years later Professor Sir George Clark, in his general introduction to the second *Cambridge Modern History*, commented on this belief of Acton and his collaborators that it would one day be possible to produce 'ultimate history', and went on:

> Historians of a later generation do not look forward to any such prospect. They expect their work to be

[1] *The Cambridge Modern History : Its Origin, Authorship and Production* (1907), pp. 10-12.

I

superseded again and again. They consider that knowledge of the past has come down through one or more human minds, has been 'processed' by them, and therefore cannot consist of elemental and impersonal atoms which nothing can alter. . . . The exploration seems to be endless, and some impatient scholars take refuge in scepticism, or at least in the doctrine that, since all historical judgments involve persons and points of view, one is as good as another and there is no 'objective' historical truth.[1]

Where the pundits contradict each other so flagrantly, the field is open to enquiry. I hope that I am sufficiently up-to-date to recognize that anything written in the 1890s must be nonsense. But I am not yet advanced enough to be committed to the view that anything written in the 1950s necessarily makes sense. Indeed, it may already have occurred to you that this enquiry is liable to stray into something even broader than the nature of history. The clash between Acton and Sir George Clark is a reflection of the change in our total outlook on society over the interval between these two pronouncements. Acton speaks out of the positive belief, the clear-eyed self-confidence, of the later Victorian age, Sir George Clark echoes the bewilderment and distracted scepticism of the beat generation. When we attempt to answer the question, What is History?, our answer, consciously or unconsciously, reflects our own position in time, and forms part of our answer to the broader question what view we take of the society in which we live. I have no fear that my subject may, on closer inspection, seem trivial. I am afraid only that I may seem presumptuous to have broached a question so vast and so important.

The nineteenth century was a great age for facts. 'What I want', said Mr. Gradgrind in *Hard Times*, 'is Facts. . . .

---

[1] *The New Cambridge Modern History*, i (1957), pp. xxiv-xxv.

Facts alone are wanted in life.' Nineteenth-century historians
on the whole agreed with him. When Ranke in the 1830s,
in legitimate protest against moralizing history, remarked
that the task of the historian was 'simply to show how it
really was (*wie es eigentlich gewesen*)', this not very profound
aphorism had an astonishing success. Three generations of
German, British and even French historians marched into
battle intoning the magic words ' *Wie es eigentlich gewesen*'
like an incantation — designed, like most incantations, to save
them from the tiresome obligation to think for themselves.
The Positivists, anxious to stake out their claim for history
as a science, contributed the weight of their influence to this
cult of facts. First ascertain the facts, said the Positivists,
then draw your conclusions from them. In Great Britain,
this view of history fitted in perfectly with the empiricist
tradition which was the dominant strain in British philosophy
from Locke to Bertrand Russell. The empirical theory of
knowledge presupposes a complete separation between subject
and object. Facts, like sense-impressions, impinge on the
observer from outside, and are independent of his consciousness. The process of reception is passive : having received
the data, he then acts on them. The Oxford Shorter English
Dictionary, a useful but tendentious work of the empirical
school, clearly marks the separateness of the two processes by
defining a fact as 'a datum of experience as distinct from conclusions'. This is what may be called the common-sense view
of history. History consists of a corpus of ascertained facts.
The facts are available to the historian in documents, inscriptions and so on, like fish on the fishmonger's slab. The
historian collects them, takes them home and cooks and serves
them in whatever style appeals to him. Acton, whose culinary
tastes were austere, wanted them served plain. In his letter
of instructions to contributors to the first *Cambridge Modern
History* he announced the requirement 'that our Waterloo
must be one that satisfies French and English, German and
Dutch alike ; that nobody can tell, without examining the list

3

of authors where the Bishop of Oxford laid down the pen, and whether Fairbairn or Gasquet, Liebermann or Harrison took it up'.[1] Even Sir George Clark, critical as he was of Acton's attitude, himself contrasted the 'hard core of facts' in history with the 'surrounding pulp of disputable interpretation'[2] — forgetting perhaps that the pulpy part of the fruit is more rewarding than the hard core. First get your facts straight, then plunge at your peril into the shifting sands of interpretation — that is the ultimate wisdom of the empirical, common-sense school of history. It recalls the favourite dictum of the great liberal journalist C. P. Scott: 'Facts are sacred, opinion is free'.

Now this clearly will not do. I shall not embark on a philosophical discussion of the nature of our knowledge of the past. Let us assume for present purposes that the fact that Caesar crossed the Rubicon and the fact there is a table in the middle of the room are facts of the same or of a comparable order, that both these facts enter our consciousness in the same or in a comparable manner, and that both have the same objective character in relation to the person who knows them. But, even on this bold and not very plausible assumption, our argument at once runs into the difficulty that not all facts about the past are historical facts, or are treated as such by the historian. What is the criterion which distinguishes the facts of history from other facts about the past?

What is a historical fact? This is a crucial question into which we must look a little more closely. According to the common-sense view, there are certain basic facts which are the same for all historians and which form, so to speak, the backbone of history — the fact, for example, that the Battle of Hastings was fought in 1066. But this view calls for two observations. In the first place, it is not with facts like these that the historian is primarily concerned. It is no doubt important to know that the great battle was fought in 1066

[1] Acton, *Lectures on Modern History* (1906), p. 318.
[2] Quoted in *The Listener*, June 19, 1952, p. 992.

and not in 1065 or 1067, and that it was fought at Hastings and not at Eastbourne or Brighton. The historian must not get these things wrong. But when points of this kind are raised, I am reminded of Housman's remark that 'accuracy is a duty, not a virtue'.[1] To praise a historian for his accuracy is like praising an architect for using well seasoned timber or properly mixed concrete in his building. It is a necessary condition of his work, but not his essential function. It is precisely for matters of this kind that the historian is entitled to rely on what have been called the 'auxiliary sciences' of history — archaeology, epigraphy, numismatics, chronology, and so forth. The historian is not required to have the special skills which enable the expert to determine the origin and period of a fragment of pottery or marble, to decypher an obscure inscription, or to make the elaborate astronomical calculations necessary to establish a precise date. These so-called basic facts which are the same for all historians commonly belong to the category of the raw materials of the historian rather than of history itself. The second observation is that the necessity to establish these basic facts rests not on any quality in the facts themselves, but on an *a priori* decision of the historian. In spite of C. P. Scott's motto, every journalist knows today that the most effective way to influence opinion is by the selection and arrangement of the appropriate facts. It used to be said that facts speak for themselves. This is, of course, untrue. The facts speak only when the historian calls on them : it is he who decides to which facts to give the floor, and in what order or context. It was, I think, one of Pirandello's characters who said that a fact is like a sack — it won't stand up till you've put something in it. The only reason why we are interested to know that the battle was fought at Hastings in 1066 is that historians regard it as a major historical event. It is the historian who has decided for his own reasons that Caesar's crossing of that petty stream, the Rubicon, is a fact of history, whereas the

[1] *M. Manilii Astronomicon : Liber Primus* (2nd ed., 1937), p. 87.

crossing of the Rubicon by millions of other people before or since interests nobody at all. The fact that you arrived in this building half an hour ago on foot, or on a bicycle, or in a car, is just as much a fact about the past as the fact that Caesar crossed the Rubicon. But it will probably be ignored by historians. Professor Talcott Parsons once called science 'a selective system of cognitive orientations to reality'.[1] It might perhaps have been put more simply. But history is, among other things, that. The historian is necessarily selective. The belief in a hard core of historical facts existing objectively and independently of the interpretation of the historian is a preposterous fallacy, but one which it is very hard to eradicate.

Let us take a look at the process by which a mere fact about the past is transformed into a fact of history. At Stalybridge Wakes in 1850, a vendor of ginger-bread, as the result of some petty dispute, was deliberately kicked to death by an angry mob. Is this a fact of history? A year ago I should unhesitatingly have said 'no'. It was recorded by an eye-witness in some little-known memoirs;[2] but I had never seen it judged worthy of mention by any historian. A year ago Dr. Kitson Clark cited it in his Ford lectures in Oxford.[3] Does this make it into a historical fact? Not, I think, yet. Its present status, I suggest, is that it has been proposed for membership of the select club of historical facts. It now awaits a seconder and sponsors. It may be that in the course of the next few years we shall see this fact appearing first in footnotes, then in the text, of articles and books about nineteenth century England, and that in twenty or thirty years' time it may be a well established historical fact. Alternatively, nobody may take it up, in which case it will relapse into the limbo of unhistorical facts about the past from which Dr.

[1] T. Parsons and E. Shils, *Towards a General Theory of Action* (3rd ed., 1954), p. 167.
[2] Lord George Sanger, *Seventy Years a Showman* (2nd ed., 1926), pp. 188-189.
[3] These will shortly be published under the title *The Making of Victorian England*.

Kitson Clark has gallantly attempted to rescue it. What will decide which of these two things will happen ? It will depend, I think, on whether the thesis or interpretation in support of which Dr. Kitson Clark cited this incident is accepted by other historians as valid and significant. Its status as a historical fact will turn on a question of interpretation. This element of interpretation enters into every fact of history.

May I be allowed a personal reminiscence ? When I studied ancient history in this university many years ago, I had as a special subject 'Greece in the period of the Persian Wars'. I collected fifteen or twenty volumes on my shelves and took it for granted that there, recorded in these volumes, I had all the facts relating to my subject. Let us assume — it was very nearly true — that those volumes contained all the facts about it that were then known, or could be known. It never occurred to me to enquire by what accident or process of attrition that minute selection of facts, out of all the myriad facts that must once have been known to somebody, had survived to become *the* facts of history. I suspect that even today one of the fascinations of ancient and mediaeval history is that it gives us the illusion of having all the facts at our disposal within a manageable compass : the nagging distinction between the facts of history and other facts about the past vanishes because the few known facts are all facts of history. As Bury who had worked in both periods said, 'the records of ancient and mediaeval history are starred with lacunae'.[1] History has been called an enormous jig-saw with a lot of missing parts. But the main trouble does not consist in the lacunae. Our picture of Greece in the fifth century B.C. is defective not primarily because so many of the bits have been accidentally lost, but because it is, by and large, the picture formed by a tiny group of people in the city of Athens. We know a lot about what fifth-century Greece looked like to an Athenian citizen ; but hardly anything about what it looked like to a Spartan, a Corinthian or a Theban —

[1] J. B. Bury, *Selected Essays* (1930), p. 52.

not to mention a Persian, or a slave or other non-citizen resident in Athens. Our picture has been pre-selected and predetermined for us, not so much by accident as by people who were consciously or unconsciously imbued with a particular view and thought the facts which supported that view worth preserving. In the same way, when I read in a modern history of the Middle Ages that the people of the Middle Ages were deeply concerned with religion, I wonder how we know this, and whether it is true. What we know as the facts of mediaeval history have almost all been selected for us by generations of chroniclers who were professionally occupied in the theory and practice of religion, and who therefore thought it supremely important, and recorded everything relating to it, and not much else. The picture of the Russian peasant as devoutly religious was destroyed by the revolution of 1917. The picture of mediaeval man as devoutly religious, whether true or not, is indestructible, because nearly all the known facts about him were pre-selected for us by people who believed it, and wanted others to believe it, and a mass of other facts, in which we might possibly have found evidence to the contrary, has been lost beyond recall. The dead hand of vanished generations of historians, scribes and chroniclers has determined beyond the possibility of appeal the pattern of the past. 'The history we read,' writes Professor Barraclough, himself trained as a mediaevalist, 'though based on facts, is, strictly speaking, not factual at all, but a series of accepted judgments.'[1]

But let us turn to the different, but equally grave, plight of the modern historian. The ancient or mediaeval historian may be grateful for the vast winnowing process which, over the years, has put at his disposal a manageable corpus of historical facts. As Lytton Strachey said in his mischievous way, 'ignorance is the first requisite of the historian, ignorance which simplifies and clarifies, which selects and omits'.[2] When

[1] G. Barraclough, *History in a Changing World* (1955), p. 14.
[2] Lytton Strachey, Preface to *Eminent Victorians*.

8

I am tempted, as I sometimes am, to envy the extreme competence of colleagues engaged in writing ancient or mediaeval history, I find consolation in the reflexion that they are so competent mainly because they are so ignorant of their subject. The modern historian enjoys none of the advantages of this built-in ignorance. He must cultivate this necessary ignorance for himself — the more so the nearer he comes to his own times. He has the dual task of discovering the few significant facts and turning them into facts of history, and of discarding the many insignificant facts as unhistorical. But this is the very converse of the nineteenth-century heresy that history consists of the compilation of a maximum number of irrefutable and objective facts. Anyone who succumbs to this heresy will either have to give up history as a bad job, and take to stamp-collecting or some other form of antiquarianism, or end in a madhouse. It is this heresy which during the past hundred years has had such devastating effects on the modern historian, producing in Germany, in Great Britain and in the United States, a vast and growing mass of dry-as-dust factual histories, of minutely specialized monographs, of would-be historians knowing more and more about less and less, sunk without trace in an ocean of facts. It was, I suspect, this heresy — rather than the alleged conflict between liberal and Catholic loyalties — which frustrated Acton as a historian. In an early essay he said of his teacher Döllinger : 'He would not write with imperfect materials, and to him the materials were always imperfect'.[1] Acton was surely here pronouncing an anticipatory verdict on himself, on that strange phenomenon of a historian whom many would regard as the most distinguished occupant the Regius Chair of Modern History in this university has ever had — but who wrote no history. And Acton wrote his own epitaph in the introductory note

---

[1] Quoted in G. P. Gooch, *History and Historians in the Nineteenth Century*, p. 385 ; later Acton said of Döllinger that 'it was given him to form his philosophy of history on the largest induction ever available to man' (*History of Freedom and Other Essays* (1907), p. 435).

to the first volume of the *Cambridge Modern History* published just after his death, when he lamented that the requirements pressing on the historian 'threaten to turn him from a man of letters into the compiler of an encyclopedia'.[1] Something had gone wrong. What had gone wrong was the belief in this untiring and unending accumulation of hard facts as the foundation of history, the belief that facts speak for themselves and that we cannot have too many facts, a belief at that time so unquestioning that few historians then thought it necessary — and some still think it unnecessary today — to ask themselves the question, What is History?

The nineteenth-century fetishism of facts was completed and justified by a fetishism of documents. The documents were the Ark of the Covenant in the temple of facts. The reverent historian approached them with bowed head and spoke of them in awed tones. If you find it in the documents, it is so. But what, when we get down to it, do these documents — the decrees, the treaties, the rent-rolls, the blue books, the official correspondence, the private letters and diaries — tell us? No document can tell us more than what the author of the document thought — what he thought had happened, what he thought ought to happen or would happen, or perhaps only what he wanted others to think he thought, or even only what he himself thought he thought. None of this means anything until the historian has got to work on it and decyphered it. The facts, whether found in documents or not, have still to be processed by the historian before he can make any use of them: the use he makes of them is, if I may put it that way, the processing process.

Let me illustrate what I am trying to say by an example which I happen to know well. When Gustav Stresemann, the Foreign Minister of the Weimar Republic, died in 1929, he left behind him an enormous mass — 300 boxes full — of papers, official, semi-official and private, nearly all relating to the six years of his tenure of office as Foreign Minister. His

[1] *Cambridge Modern History*, i (1902), 4.

friends and relatives naturally thought that a monument should be raised to the memory of so great a man. His faithful secretary Bernhard got to work ; and within three years there appeared three massive volumes, of some 600 pages each, of selected documents from the 300 boxes with the impressive title *Stresemanns Vermächtnis*. In the ordinary way the documents themselves would have mouldered away in some cellar or attic and disappeared for ever ; or perhaps in a hundred years or so some curious scholar would have come upon them and set out to compare them with Bernhard's text. What happened was far more dramatic. In 1945 the documents fell into the hands of the British and American Governments, who photographed the lot and put the photostats at the disposal of scholars in the Public Record Office in London and in the National Archives in Washington, so that, if we have sufficient patience and curiosity, we can discover exactly what Bernhard did. What he did was neither very unusual nor very shocking. When Stresemann died, his western policy seemed to have been crowned with a series of brilliant successes — Locarno, the admission of Germany to the League of Nations, the Dawes and Young plans and the American loans, the withdrawal of allied occupation armies from the Rhineland. This seemed the important and rewarding part of Stresemann's foreign policy ; and it was not unnatural that it should have been over-represented in Bernhard's selection of documents. Stresemann's eastern policy, on the other hand, his relations with the Soviet Union, seemed to have led nowhere in particular ; and, since masses of documents about negotiations which yielded only trivial results were not very interesting and added nothing to Stresemann's reputation, the process of selection could be more rigorous. Stresemann in fact devoted a far more constant and anxious attention to relations with the Soviet Union, and they played a far larger part in his foreign policy as a whole, than the reader of the Bernhard selection would surmise. But the Bernhard volumes compare favourably, I suspect, with many published collections of documents on which the ordinary historian implicitly relies.

This is not the end of my story. Shortly after the publication of Bernhard's volumes, Hitler came into power. Stresemann's name was consigned to oblivion in Germany, and the volumes disappeared from circulation : many, perhaps most, of the copies must have been destroyed. Today *Stresemanns Vermächtnis* is a rather rare book. But in the west Stresemann's reputation stood high. In 1935 an English publisher brought out an abbreviated translation of Bernhard's work — a selection from Bernhard's selection; perhaps one-third of the original was omitted. Sutton, a well-known translator from the German, did his job competently and well. The English version, he explained in the preface, was 'slightly condensed, but only by the omission of a certain amount of what, it was felt, was more ephemeral matter . . . of little interest to English readers or students'.[1] This again is natural enough. But the result is that Stresemann's eastern policy, already under-represented in Bernhard, recedes still further from view, and the Soviet Union appears in Sutton's volumes merely as an occasional and rather unwelcome intruder in Stresemann's predominantly western foreign policy. Yet it is safe to say that, for all except a few specialists, Sutton and not Bernhard — and still less the documents themselves — represents for the western world the authentic voice of Stresemann. Had the documents perished in 1945 in the bombing, and had the remaining Bernhard volumes disappeared, the authenticity and authority of Sutton would never have been questioned. Many printed collections of documents gratefully accepted by historians in default of the originals rest on no securer basis than this.

But I want to carry the story one step further. Let us forget about Bernhard and Sutton, and be thankful that we can, if we choose, consult the authentic papers of a leading

[1] *Gustav Stresemann, His Diaries, Letters and Papers*, i (1935), Editor's Note.

participant in some important events of recent European history. What do the papers tell us? Among other things they contain records of some hundreds of Stresemann's conversations with the Soviet Ambassador in Berlin and of a score or so with Chicherin. These records have one feature in common. They depict Stresemann as having the lion's share of the conversations and reveal his arguments as invariably well put and cogent, while those of his partner are for the most part scanty, confused and unconvincing. This is a familiar characteristic of all records of diplomatic conversations. The documents do not tell us what happened, but only what Stresemann thought had happened, or what he wanted others to think, or perhaps what he wanted himself to think, had happened. It was not Sutton or Bernhard, but Stresemann himself, who started the process of selection. And if we had, say, Chicherin's records of these same conversations, we should still learn from them only what Chicherin thought, and what really happened would still have to be reconstructed in the mind of the historian. Of course, facts and documents are essential to the historian. But do not make a fetish of them. They do not by themselves constitute history; they provide in themselves no ready-made answer to this tiresome question, What is History?

At this point I should like to say a few words on the question why nineteenth-century historians were generally indifferent to the philosophy of history. The term was invented by Voltaire, and has since been used in different senses; but I shall take it to mean, if I use it at all, our answer to the question, What is History? The nineteenth century was, for the intellectuals of western Europe, a comfortable period exuding confidence and optimism. The facts were on the whole satisfactory; and the inclination to ask and answer awkward questions about them was correspondingly weak. Ranke piously believed that divine providence would take care of the meaning of history if he took care of the facts; and Burckhardt with a more modern touch of cynicism observed that 'we are not initiated into the purposes of the eternal wisdom'. Professor Butterfield as late as 1931 noted with apparent satisfaction that 'historians have reflected little upon the nature of things and even the nature of their own subject'.[1] But my predecessor in these lectures, Dr. A. L. Rowse, more justly critical, wrote of Sir Winston Churchill's *World Crisis* — his book about the first World War — that, while it matched Trotsky's *History of the Russian Revolution* in personality, vividness and vitality, it was inferior in one respect: it had 'no philosophy of history behind it'.[2] British historians refused to be drawn, not because they believed that history had no meaning, but because they believed that its meaning was implicit and self-evident. The liberal nineteenth-century view of history had a close affinity with the economic doctrine of *laissez-faire* — also the product of a serene and self-confident outlook on the world. Let everyone get on with his particular job, and the hidden hand would take care of the universal harmony. The facts of history were themselves a demonstration of the supreme fact of a beneficent and apparently infinite progress towards higher things. This was the age of innocence, and historians walked in the Garden of Eden, without a scrap of philosophy to cover them, naked and unashamed before the god of history. Since then, we have known Sin and experienced a Fall; and those historians who today pretend to dispense with a philosophy of history are merely trying, vainly and self-consciously, like members of a nudist colony, to recreate the Garden of Eden in their garden suburb. Today the awkward question can no longer be evaded.

During the past fifty years a good deal of serious work has been done on the question, *What is History?* It was from Germany, the country which was to do so much to upset the

[1] H. Butterfield, *The Whig Interpretation of History* (1931), p. 67.
[2] A. L. Rowse, *The End of an Epoch* (1947), pp. 282-283.

comfortable reign of nineteenth-century liberalism, that the first challenge came in the 1880s and 1890s to the doctrine of the primacy and autonomy of facts in history. The philosophers who made the challenge are now little more than names : Dilthey is the only one of them who has recently received some belated recognition in Great Britain. Before the turn of the century, prosperity and confidence were still too great in this country for any attention to be paid to heretics who attacked the cult of facts. But early in the new century, the torch passed to Italy, where Croce began to propound a philosophy of history which obviously owed much to German masters. All history is 'contemporary history', declared Croce,[1] meaning that history consists essentially in seeing the past through the eyes of the present and in the light of its problems, and that the main work of the historian is not to record, but to evaluate ; for, if he does not evaluate, how can he know what is worth recording ? In 1910 the American historian, Carl Becker, argued in deliberately provocative language that 'the facts of history do not exist for any historian till he creates them'.[2] These challenges were for the moment little noticed. It was only after 1920 that Croce began to have a considerable vogue in France and Great Britain. This was not perhaps because Croce was a subtler thinker or a better stylist than his German predecessors, but because, after the first World War, the facts seemed to smile on us less propitiously than in the years before 1914, and we were therefore more accessible to a philosophy which sought to diminish their prestige. Croce was an important influence on the Oxford philosopher and historian Collingwood, the only

[1] The context of this celebrated aphorism is as follows : 'The practical requirements which underlie every historical judgment give to all history the character of "contemporary history", because, however remote in time events thus recounted may seem to be, the history in reality refers to present needs and present situations wherein those events vibrate' (B. Croce, *History as the Story of Liberty* (Engl. transl., 1941), p. 19.
[2] *Atlantic Monthly*, October 1910, p. 528.

British thinker in the present century who has made a serious contribution to the philosophy of history. He did not live to write the systematic treatise he had planned ; but his published and unpublished papers on the subject were collected after his death in a volume entitled *The Idea of History*, which appeared in 1945.

The views of Collingwood can be summarized as follows. The philosophy of history is concerned neither with 'the past by itself' nor with 'the historian's thought about it by itself', but with 'the two things in their mutual relations'. (This dictum reflects the two current meanings of the word 'history' — the enquiry conducted by the historian and the series of past events into which he enquires.) 'The past which an historian studies is not a dead past, but a past which in some sense is still living in the present.' But a past act is dead, *i.e.* meaningless to the historian, unless he can understand the thought that lay behind it. Hence 'all history is the history of thought', and 'history is the re-enactment in the historian's mind of the thought whose history he is studying'. The reconstitution of the past in the historian's mind is dependent on empirical evidence. But it is not in itself an empirical process, and cannot consist in a mere recital of facts. On the contrary, the process of reconstitution governs the selection and interpretation of the facts : this, indeed, is what makes them historical facts. 'History', says Professor Oakeshott who on this point stands near to Collingwood, 'is the historian's experience. It is "made" by nobody save the historian : to write history is the only way of making it.'[1]

This searching critique, though it may call for some serious reservations, brings to light certain neglected truths.

In the first place, the facts of history never come to us 'pure', since they do not and cannot exist in a pure form : they are always refracted through the mind of the recorder. It follows that when we take up a work of history, our first concern should be not with the facts which it contains but

[1] M. Oakeshott, *Experience and Its Modes* (1933), p. 99.

with the historian who wrote it. Let me take as an example the great historian in whose honour and in whose name these lectures were founded. Trevelyan, as he tells us in his autobiography, was 'brought up at home on a somewhat exuberantly Whig tradition';[1] and he would not, I hope, disclaim the title if I described him as the last and not the least of the great English liberal historians of the Whig tradition. It is not for nothing that he traces back his family tree, through the great Whig historian George Otto Trevelyan, to Macaulay, incomparably the greatest of the Whig historians. Dr. Trevelyan's finest and maturest work *England under Queen Anne* was written against that background, and will yield its full meaning and significance to the reader only when read against that background. The author, indeed, leaves the reader with no excuse for failing to do so. For if, following the technique of connoisseurs of detective novels, you read the end first, you will find on the last few pages of the third volume the best summary known to me of what is nowadays called the Whig interpretation of history ; and you will see that what Trevelyan is trying to do is to investigate the origin and development of the Whig tradition, and to root it fairly and squarely in the years after the death of its founder, William III. Though this is not, perhaps, the only conceivable interpretation of the events of Queen Anne's reign, it is a valid and, in Trevelyan's hands, a fruitful interpretation. But, in order to appreciate it at its full value, you have to understand what the historian is doing. For if, as Collingwood says, the historian must re-enact in thought what has gone on in the mind of his *dramatis personae*, so the reader in his turn must re-enact what goes on in the mind of the historian. Study the historian before you begin to study the facts. This is, after all, not very abstruse. It is what is already done by the intelligent undergraduate who, when recommended to read a work by that great scholar Jones of St. Jude's, goes round to a friend at St. Jude's to ask what sort of chap Jones is, and

[1] G. M. Trevelyan, *An Autobiography* (1949), p. 11.

what bees he has in his bonnet. When you read a work of history, always listen out for the buzzing. If you can detect none, either you are tone deaf or your historian is a dull dog. The facts are really not at all like fish on the fishmonger's slab. They are like fish swimming about in a vast and sometimes inaccessible ocean ; and what the historian catches will depend, partly on chance, but mainly on what part of the ocean he chooses to fish in and what tackle he chooses to use — these two factors being, of course, determined by the kind of fish he wants to catch. By and large, the historian will get the kind of facts he wants. History means interpretation. Indeed, if, standing Sir George Clark on his head, I were to call history 'a hard core of interpretation surrounded by a pulp of disputable facts', my statement would, no doubt, be one-sided and misleading, but no more so, I venture to think, than the original dictum.

The second point is the more familiar one of the historian's need of imaginative understanding for the minds of the people with whom he is dealing, for the thought behind their acts : I say 'imaginative understanding', not 'sympathy', lest sympathy should be supposed to imply agreement. The nineteenth century was weak in mediaeval history, because it was too much repelled by the superstitious beliefs of the Middle Ages and by the barbarities which they inspired, to have any imaginative understanding of mediaeval people. Or take Burckhardt's censorious remark about the Thirty Years War : 'It is scandalous for a creed, no matter whether it is Catholic or Protestant, to place its salvation above the integrity of the nation'.[1] It was extremely difficult for a nineteenth-century liberal historian, brought up to believe that it is right and praiseworthy to kill in defence of one's country, but wicked and wrong-headed to kill in defence of one's religion, to enter into the state of mind of those who fought the Thirty Years War. This difficulty is particularly acute in the field in which I am now working. Much of what has been written in English-

[1] J. Burckhardt, *Judgements on History and Historians* (1959), p. 179.

speaking countries in the last ten years about the Soviet Union, and in the Soviet Union about the English-speaking countries, has been vitiated by this inability to achieve even the most elementary measure of imaginative understanding of what goes on in the mind of the other party, so that the words and actions of the other are always made to appear malign, senseless or hypocritical. History cannot be written unless the historian can achieve some kind of contact with the mind of those about whom he is writing.

The third point is that we can view the past, and achieve our understanding of the past, only through the eyes of the present. The historian is of his own age, and is bound to it by the conditions of human existence. The very words which he uses — words like democracy, empire, war, revolution — have current connotations from which he cannot divorce them. Ancient historians have taken to using words like *polis* and *plebs* in the original, just in order to show that they have not fallen into this trap. This does not help them. They, too, live in the present, and cannot cheat themselves into the past by using unfamiliar or obsolete words, any more than they would become better Greek or Roman historians if they delivered their lectures in a *chlamys* or a *toga*. The names by which successive French historians have described the Parisian crowds which played so prominent a role in the French revolution — *les sans-culottes, le peuple, la canaille, les bras-nus* — are all, for those who know the rules of the game, manifestos of a political affiliation and of a particular interpretation. Yet the historian is obliged to choose : the use of language forbids him to be neutral. Nor is it a matter of words alone. Over the past hundred years the changed balance of power in Europe has reversed the attitude of British historians to Frederick the Great. The changed balance of power within the Christian churches between Catholicism and Protestantism has profoundly altered their attitude to such figures as Loyola, Luther and Cromwell. It requires only a superficial knowledge of the work of French historians of the last forty years on the French revolution to recognize how deeply it has been affected by the Russian revolution of 1917. The historian belongs not to the past but to the present. Professor Trevor-Roper tells us that the historian 'ought to love the past'.[1] This is a dubious injunction. To love the past may easily be an expression of the nostalgic romanticism of old men and old societies, a symptom of loss of faith and interest in the present or future.[2] Cliché for cliché, I should prefer the one about freeing oneself from 'the dead hand of the past'. The function of the historian is neither to love the past nor to emancipate himself from the past, but to master and understand it as the key to the understanding of the present.

If, however, these are some of the insights of what I may call the Collingwood view of history, it is time to consider some of the dangers. The emphasis on the role of the historian in the making of history tends, if pressed to its logical conclusion, to rule out any objective history at all: history is what the historian makes. Collingwood seems indeed, at one moment, in an unpublished note quoted by his editor, to have reached this conclusion:

> St. Augustine looked at history from the point of view of the early Christian; Tillamont, from that of a seventeenth century Frenchman; Gibbon, from that of an eighteenth century Englishman; Mommsen from that of a nineteenth century German. There is no point in asking which was the right point of view. Each was the only one possible for the man who adopted it.[3]

[1] Introduction to J. Burckhardt, *Judgements on History and Historians* (1959), p. 17.
[2] Compare Nietzsche's view of history: 'To old age belongs the old man's business of looking back and casting up his accounts, of seeking consolation in the memories of the past, in historical culture' (*Thoughts Out of Season* (Engl. transl., 1909), ii, 65-66).
[3] R. Collingwood, *The Idea of History* (1946), p. xii.

This amounts to total scepticism, like Froude's remark that history is 'a child's box of letters with which we can spell any word we please'.[1] Collingwood, in his reaction against 'scissors-and-paste history', against the view of history as a mere compilation of facts, comes perilously near to treating history as something spun out of the human brain, and leads back to the conclusion referred to by Sir George Clark in the passage which I quoted earlier, that 'there is no "objective" historical truth'. In place of the theory that history has no meaning, we are offered here the theory of an infinity of meanings, none any more right than any other — which comes to much the same thing. The second theory is surely as untenable as the first. It does not follow that, because a mountain appears to take on different shapes from different angles of vision, it has objectively either no shape at all or an infinity of shapes. It does not follow that, because interpretation plays a necessary part in establishing the facts of history, and because no existing interpretation is wholly objective, one interpretation is as good as another, and the facts of history are in principle not amenable to objective interpretation. I shall have to consider at a later stage what exactly is meant by objectivity in history.

But a still greater danger lurks in the Collingwood hypothesis. If the historian necessarily looks at his period of history through the eyes of his own time, and studies the problems of the past as a key to those of the present, will he not fall into a purely pragmatic view of the facts, and maintain that the criterion of a right interpretation is its suitability to some present purpose? On this hypothesis, the facts of history are nothing, interpretation is everything. Nietzsche had already enunciated the principle: 'The falseness of an opinion is not for us any objection to it. . . . The question is how far it is life-furthering, life-preserving, species-preserving, perhaps species-creating'.[2] The American pragmatists, moved,

[1] A. Froude, *Short Studies on Great Subjects*, i (1894), 21.
[2] *Beyond Good and Evil*, ch. i.

less explicitly and less wholeheartedly, along the same line. Knowledge is knowledge for some purpose. The validity of the knowledge depends on the validity of the purpose. But, even where no such theory has been professed, the practice has often been no less disquieting. In my own field of study I have seen too many examples of extravagant interpretation riding roughshod over facts not to be impressed with the reality of this danger. It is not surprising that perusal of some of the more extreme products of Soviet and anti-Soviet schools of historiography should sometimes breed a certain nostalgia for that illusory nineteenth-century haven of purely factual history.

How then, in the middle of the twentieth century, are we to define the obligation of the historian to his facts? I trust that I have spent a sufficient number of hours in recent years chasing and perusing documents, and stuffing my historical narrative with properly footnoted facts, to escape the imputation of treating facts and documents too cavalierly. The duty of the historian to respect his facts is not exhausted by the obligation to see that his facts are accurate. He must seek to bring into the picture all known or knowable facts relevant, in one sense or another, to the theme on which he is engaged and to the interpretation proposed. If he seeks to depict the Victorian Englishman as a moral and rational being, he must not forget what happened at Stalybridge Wakes in 1850. But this, in turn, does not mean that he can eliminate interpretation, which is the life-blood of history. Laymen — that is to say, non-academic friends or friends from other academic disciplines — sometimes ask me how the historian goes to work when he writes history. The commonest assumption appears to be that the historian divides his work into two sharply distinguishable phases or periods. First, he spends a long preliminary period reading his sources and filling his notebooks with facts : then, when this is over, he puts away his sources, takes out his notebooks and writes his book from beginning to end. This is to me an unconvincing and unplausible picture. For myself, as soon as I have got going on a few of what I take to be the capital sources, the itch becomes too strong and I begin to write — not necessarily at the beginning, but somewhere, anywhere. Thereafter, reading and writing go on simultaneously. The writing is added to, subtracted from, re-shaped, cancelled, as I go on reading. The reading is guided and directed and made fruitful by the writing: the more I write, the more I know what I am looking for, the better I understand the significance and revelance of what I find. Some historians probably do all this preliminary writing in their head without using pen, paper or typewriter, just as some people play chess in their heads without recourse to board and chess-men: this is a talent which I envy, but cannot emulate. But I am convinced that, for any historian worth the name, the two processes of what economists call 'input' and 'output' go on simultaneously and are, in practice, parts of a single process. If you try to separate them, or to give one priority over the other, you fall into one of two heresies. Either you write scissors-and-paste history without meaning or significance; or you write propaganda or historical fiction, and merely use facts of the past to embroider a kind of writing which has nothing to do with history.

Our examination of the relation of the historian to the facts of history finds us, therefore, in an apparently precarious situation, navigating delicately between the Scylla of an untenable theory of history as an objective compilation of facts, of the unqualified primacy of fact over interpretation, and the Charybdis of an equally untenable theory of history as the subjective product of the mind of the historian who establishes the facts of history and masters them through the process of interpretation, between a view of history having the centre of gravity in the past and a view having the centre of gravity in the present. But our situation is less precarious than it seems. We shall encounter the same dichotomy of fact and interpretation again in these lectures in other guises — the particular and the general, the empirical and the theoretical, the objective and the subjective. The predicament of the historian is a reflexion of the nature of man. Man, except perhaps in earliest infancy and in extreme old age, is not totally involved in his environment and unconditionally subject to it. On the other hand, he is never totally independent of it and its unconditional master. The relation of man to his environment is the relation of the historian to his theme. The historian is neither the humble slave, nor the tyrannical master, of his facts. The relation between the historian and his facts is one of equality, of give-and-take. As any working historian knows, if he stops to reflect what he is doing as he thinks and writes, the historian is engaged on a continuous process of moulding his facts to his interpretation and his interpretation to his facts. It is impossible to assign primacy to one over the other.

The historian starts with a provisional selection of facts and a provisional interpretation in the light of which that selection has been made — by others as well as by himself. As he works, both the interpretation and the selection and ordering of facts undergo subtle and perhaps partly unconscious changes through the reciprocal action of one or the other. And this reciprocal action also involves reciprocity between present and past, since the historian is part of the present and the facts belong to the past. The historian and the facts of history are necessary to one another. The historian without his facts is rootless and futile ; the facts without their historian are dead and meaningless. My first answer therefore to the question, What is History ?, is that it is a continuous process of interaction between the historian and his facts, an unending dialogue between the present and the past.

# II

## *Society and the Individual*

THE question which comes first — society or the individual — is like the question about the hen and the egg. Whether you treat it as a logical or as an historical question, you can make no statement about it, one way or the other, which does not have to be corrected by an opposite, and equally one-sided, statement. Society and the individual are inseparable ; they are necessary and complementary to each other, not opposites. 'No man is an island, entire of itself', in Donne's famous words ; 'every man is a piece of the continent, a part of the main.'[1] That is an aspect of the truth. On the other hand, take the dictum of J. S. Mill, the classical individualist : 'Men are not, when brought together, converted into another kind of substance'.[2] Of course not. But the fallacy is to suppose that they existed, or had any kind of substance, before being 'brought together'. As soon as we are born, the world gets to work on us and transforms us from merely biological into social units. Every human being at every stage of history or pre-history is born into a society and from his earliest years is moulded by that society. The language which he speaks is not an individual inheritance, but a social acquisition from the group in which he grows up. Both language and environment help to determine the character of his thought ; his earliest ideas come to him from others. As has been well said, the individual apart from society would be both speechless and mindless. The lasting fascination of the Robinson Crusoe myth is due to its attempt to

[1] *Devotions upon Emergent Occasions*, No. xvii.
[2] J. S. Mill, *A System of Logic*, vii, l.

imagine an individual independent of society. The attempt breaks down. Robinson is not an abstract individual, but an Englishman from York; he carries his Bible with him and prays to his tribal God. The myth quickly bestows on him his Man Friday; and the building of a new society begins. The other relevant myth is that of Kirillov in Dostoevsky's *Devils* who kills himself in order to demonstrate his perfect freedom. Suicide is the only perfectly free act open to individual man; every other act involves in one way or another his membership of society.[1]

It is commonly said by anthropologists that primitive man is less individual and more completely moulded by his society than civilized man. This contains an element of truth. Simpler societies are more uniform in the sense that they call for, and provide opportunities for, a far smaller diversity of individual skills and occupations than the more complex and advanced societies. Increasing individualization in this sense is a necessary product of modern advanced society, and runs through all its activities from top to bottom. But it would be a serious error to set up an antithesis between this process of individualization and the growing strength and cohesion of society. The development of society and the development of the individual go hand in hand, and condition each other. Indeed what we mean by a complex or advanced society is a society in which the interdependence of individuals on one another has assumed advanced and complex forms. It would be dangerous to assume that the power of a modern national community to mould the character and thought of its individual members, and to produce a certain degree of conformity and uniformity among them, is any less than that of a primitive tribal community. The old conception of national character based on biological differences has long been exploded; but

[1] Durkheim, in his well-known study of suicide, coined the word *anomie* to denote the condition of the individual isolated from his society — a state especially conducive to emotional disturbance and suicide; but he also showed that suicide is by no means independent of social conditions.

differences of national character arising out of different national backgrounds of society and education are difficult to deny. That elusive entity 'human nature' has varied so much from country to country and from century to century that it is difficult not to regard it as an historical phenomenon shaped by prevailing social conditions and conventions. There are many differences between, say, Americans, Russians and Indians. But some, and perhaps the most important, of these differences take the form of different attitudes to social relations between individuals, or, in other words, to the way in which society should be constituted, so that the study of differences between American, Russian and Indian society as a whole may well turn out to be the best way of studying differences between individual Americans, Russians and Indians. Civilized man, like primitive man, is moulded by society just as effectively as society is moulded by him. You can no more have the egg without the hen than you can have the hen without the egg.

It would have been unnecessary to dwell on these very obvious truths but for the fact that they have been obscured for us by the remarkable and exceptional period of history from which the western world is only just emerging. The cult of individualism is one of the most pervasive of modern historical myths. According to the familiar account in Burckhardt's *Civilization of the Renaissance in Italy*, the second part of which is sub-titled 'The Development of the Individual', the cult of the individual began with the Renaissance, when man, who had hitherto been 'conscious of himself only as a member of a race, people, party, family or corporation', at length 'became a spiritual individual and recognized himself as such'. Later the cult was connected with the rise of capitalism and of Protestantism, with the beginnings of the industrial revolution and with the doctrines of *laissez-faire*. The rights of man and the citizen proclaimed by the French revolution were the rights of the individual. Individualism was the basis of the great nineteenth-century philosophy of utilitarianism.

Morley's essay *On Compromise*, a characteristic document of Victorian liberalism, called individualism and utilitarianism 'the religion of human happiness and well-being'. 'Rugged individualism' was the keynote of human progress. This may be a perfectly sound and valid analysis of the ideology of a particular historical epoch. But what I want to make clear is that the increased individualization which accompanied the rise of the modern world was a normal process of advancing civilization. A social revolution brought new social groups to positions of power. It operated as always through individuals and by offering fresh opportunities of individual development; and, since in the early stages of capitalism the units of production and distribution were largely in the hands of single individuals, the ideology of the new social order strongly emphasized the role of individual initiative in the social order. But the whole process was a social process representing a specific stage in historical development, and cannot be explained in terms of a revolt of individuals against society or of an emancipation of individuals from social restraints.

Many signs suggest that, even in the western world which was the focus of this development and of this ideology, this period of history has reached its end: I need not insist here on the rise of what is called mass democracy, or on the gradual replacement of predominantly individual by predominantly collective forms of economic production and organization. But the ideology generated by this long and fruitful period is still a dominant force in Western Europe and throughout the English-speaking countries. When we speak in abstract terms of the tension between liberty and equality, or between individual liberty and social justice, we are apt to forget that fights do not occur between abstract ideas. These are not struggles between individuals as such and society as such, but between groups of individuals in society, each group striving to promote social policies favourable to it and to frustrate social policies inimical to it. Individualism, in the sense no longer of a great social movement, but of false opposition between individual and society, has become today the slogan of an interested group and, because of its controversial character, a barrier to our understanding of what goes on in the world. I have nothing to say against the cult of the individual as a protest against the perversion which treats the individual as a means and society or the state as the end. But we shall arrive at no real understanding either of the past or of the present if we attempt to operate with the concept of an abstract individual standing outside society.

And this brings me at last to the point of my long digression. The common-sense view of history treats it as something written by individuals about individuals. This view was certainly taken and encouraged by nineteenth-century liberal historians, and is not in substance incorrect. But it now seems over-simplified and inadequate, and we need to probe deeper. The knowledge of the historian is not his exclusive individual possession : men, probably, of many generations and of many different countries have participated in accumulating it. The men whose actions the historian studies were not isolated individuals acting in a vacuum : they acted in the context, and under the impulse, of a past society. In my last lecture I described history as a process of interaction, a dialogue between the historian in the present and the facts of the past. I now want to enquire into the relative weight of the individual and social elements on both sides of the equation. How far are historians single individuals, and how far products of their society and their period ? How far are the facts of history facts about single individuals and how far social facts ?

The historian, then, is an individual human being. Like other individuals, he is also a social phenomenon, both the product and the conscious or unconscious spokesman of the society to which he belongs ; it is in this capacity that he approaches the facts of the historical past. We sometimes speak of the course of history as a 'moving procession'. The metaphor is fair enough, provided it does not tempt the historian to think of himself as an eagle surveying the scene from a lonely crag or as a V.I.P. at the saluting base. Nothing of the kind! The historian is just another dim figure trudging along in another part of the procession. And as the procession winds along, swerving now to the right and now to the left, and sometimes doubling back on itself, the relative positions of different parts of the procession are constantly changing, so that it may make perfectly good sense to say, for example, that we are nearer today to the Middle Ages than were our great-grandfathers a century ago, or that the age of Caesar is nearer to us than the age of Dante. New vistas, new angles of vision, constantly appear as the procession — and the historian with it — moves along. The historian is part of history. The point in the procession at which he finds himself determines his angle of vision over the past.

This truism is not less true when the period treated by the historian is remote from his own time. When I studied ancient history, the classics on the subject were — and probably still are — Grote's *History of Greece* and Mommsen's *History of Rome.* Grote, an enlightened radical banker writing in the 1840s, embodied the aspirations of the rising and politically progressive British middle class in an idealized picture of Athenian democracy, in which Pericles figured as a Benthamite reformer, and Athens acquired an empire in a fit of abscence of mind. It may not be fanciful to suggest that Grote's neglect of the problem of slavery in Athens reflected the failure of the group to which he belonged to face the problem of the new English factory working class. Mommsen was a German liberal, disillusioned by the muddles and humiliations of the German revolution of 1848–1849. Writing in the 1850s — the decade which saw the birth of the name and concept of *Realpolitik* — Mommsen was imbued with the sense of need for a strong man to clear up the mess left by the failure of the German people to realize its political aspirations ;

and we shall never appreciate his history at its true value unless we realize that his well-known idealization of Caesar is the product of this yearning for the strong man to save Germany from ruin, and that the lawyer-politician Cicero, that ineffective chatterbox and slippery procrastinator, has walked straight out of the debates of the Paulikirche in Frankfurt in 1848. Indeed, I should not think it an outrageous paradox if someone were to say that Grote's *History of Greece* has quite as much to tell us today about the thought of the English philosophical radicals in the 1840s as about Athenian democracy in the fifth century B.C., or that anyone wishing to understand what 1848 did to the German liberals should take Mommsen's *History of Rome* as one of his text-books. Nor does this diminish their stature as great historical works. I have no patience with the fashion set by Bury in his inaugural lecture of pretending that Mommsen's greatness rests not on his *History of Rome*, but on his corpus of inscriptions and his work on Roman constitutional law : this is to reduce history to the level of compilation. Great history is written precisely when the historian's vision of the past is illuminated by insights into the problems of the present. Surprise has often been expressed that Mommsen failed to continue his history beyond the fall of the republic. He lacked neither time, nor opportunity nor knowledge. But, when Mommsen wrote his history, the strong man had not yet arisen in Germany. During his active career, the problem of what happened once the strong man had taken over was not yet actual. Nothing inspired Mommsen to project this problem back on to the Roman scene ; and the history of the empire remained unwritten.

It would be easy to multiply examples of this phenomenon among modern historians. In my last lecture I paid tribute to Dr. Trevelyan's *England under Queen Anne* as a monument to the Whig tradition in which he had been reared. Let us now consider the imposing and significant achievement of one whom most of us would regard as the greatest British historian to emerge on the academic scene since the first World War: Sir Lewis Namier. Namier was a true conservative — not a typical English conservative who when scratched turns out to be 75 per cent a liberal, but a conservative such as we have not seen among British historians for more than a hundred years. Between the middle of the last century and 1914 it was scarcely possible for a British historian to conceive of historical change except as change for the better. In the 1920s, we moved into a period in which change was beginning to be associated with fear for the future, and could be thought of as change for the worse — a period of the rebirth of conservative thinking. Like Acton's liberalism, Namier's conservatism derived both strength and profundity from being rooted in a continental background.[1] Unlike Fisher or Toynbee, Namier had no roots in the nineteenth-century liberalism, and suffered from no nostalgic regrets for it. After the first World War and the abortive peace had revealed the bankruptcy of liberalism, the reaction would come only in one of two forms — socialism or conservatism. Namier appeared as the conservative historian. He worked in two chosen fields, and the choice of both was significant. In English history he went back to the last period in which the ruling class had been able to engage in the rational pursuit of position and power in an orderly and mainly static society. Somebody has accused Namier of taking mind out of history.[2] It is not perhaps a very fortunate phrase, but one can see the point which the critic was trying to make. Politics at the accession of George III were still immune from the fanaticism of ideas, and of that passionate

[1] It is perhaps worth remarking that the only other considerable conservative British writer of the period between the wars, Mr. T. S. Eliot, also enjoyed the advantage of a non-British background; nobody brought up in Great Britain before 1914 could wholly escape the inhibiting influences of the liberal tradition.

[2] The original criticism, in an anonymous article in *The Times Literary Supplement* of August 28, 1953, on 'The Namier View of History' ran as follows: 'Darwin was accused of taking mind out of the universe; and Sir Lewis has been the Darwin of political history — in more senses than one'.

belief in progress, which was to break on the world with the French revolution and usher in the century of triumphant liberalism. No ideas, no revolution, no liberalism : Namier chose to give us a brilliant portrait of an age still safe — though not to remain safe for long — from all these dangers.

But Namier's choice of a second subject was equally significant. Namier by-passed the great modern revolutions, English, French and Russian — he wrote nothing of substance on any of them — and elected to give us a penetrating study of the European revolution of 1848 — a revolution that failed, a set-back all over Europe for the rising hopes of liberalism, a demonstration of the hollowness of ideas in face of armed force, of democrats when confronted with soldiers. The intrusion of ideas into the serious business of politics is futile and dangerous : Namier rubbed in the moral by calling this humiliating failure 'the revolution of the intellectuals'. Nor is our conclusion a matter of inference alone; for, though Namier wrote nothing systematic on the philosophy of history, he expressed himself in an essay published a few years ago with his usual clarity and incisiveness. 'The less, therefore,' he wrote, 'man clogs the free play of his mind with political doctrine and dogma, the better for his thinking.' And, after mentioning, and not rejecting, the charge that he had taken the mind out of history, he went on :

> Some political philosophers complain of a 'tired lull' and the absence at present of argument on general politics in this country; practical solutions are sought for concrete problems, while programmes and ideals are forgotten by both parties. But to me this attitude seems to betoken a greater national maturity, and I can only wish that it may long continue undisturbed by the workings of political philosophy.[1]

I do not want at the moment to join issue with this view : I will reserve that for a later lecture. My purpose here is merely

---

[1] L. Namier, *Personalities and Powers* (1955), pp. 5, 7.

to illustrate two important truths : first, that you cannot fully understand or appreciate the work of the historian unless you have first grasped the standpoint from which he himself approached it ; secondly, that that standpoint is itself rooted in a social and historical background. Do not forget that, as Marx once said, the educator himself has to be educated ; in modern jargon, the brain of the brain-washer has itself been washed. The historian, before he begins to write history, is the product of history.

The historians of whom I have just spoken — Grote and Mommsen, Trevelyan and Namier — were each of them cast, so to speak, in a single social and political mould ; no marked change of outlook occurs between their earlier and later work. But some historians in periods of rapid change have reflected in their writings not one society and one social order, but a succession of different orders. The best example known to me of this is the great German historian Meinecke, whose span of life and work was unusually long, and covered a series of revolutionary and catastrophic changes in the fortunes of his country. Here we have in effect three different Meineckes, each the spokesman of a different historical epoch, and each speaking through one of his three major works. The Meinecke of *Weltbürgerthum and Nationalstaat*, published in 1907, confidently sees the realization of German national ideals in the Bismarckian Reich and — like many nineteenth-century thinkers from Mazzini onwards — identifies nationalism with the highest form of universalism : this is the product of the baroque Wilhelmine sequel to the age of Bismarck. The Meinecke of *Die Idee der Staatsräson*, published in 1925, speaks with the divided and bewildered mind of the Weimar republic : the world of politics has become an arena of unresolved conflict between *raison d'état* and a morality which is external to politics, but which cannot in the last resort override the life and security of the state. Finally the Meinecke of *Die Entstehung des Historismus*, published in 1936 when he had been swept from his academic honours by the Nazi

flood, utters a cry of despair, rejecting a historicism which
appears to recognize that whatever is, is right, and tossing
uneasily between the historical relative and a super-rational
absolute. Last of all, when Meinecke in his old age had seen
his country succumb to a military defeat more crushing than
that of 1918, he relapsed helplessly in *Die Deutsche Katastrophe*
of 1946 into the belief in a history at the mercy of blind, inexorable chance.[1] The psychologist or the biographer would
be interested here in Meinecke's development as an individual :
what interests the historian is the way in which Meinecke
reflects back three — or even four — successive, and sharply
contrasted, periods of present time into the historical past.

Or let us take a distinguished example nearer home. In
the iconoclastic 1930s, when the Liberal Party had just been
snuffed out as an effective force in British politics, Professor
Butterfield wrote a book called *The Whig Interpretation of
History*, which enjoyed a great and deserved success. It was
a remarkable book in many ways — not least because, though
it denounced the Whig Interpretation over some 130 pages,
it did not, so far as I can discover without the help of an index,
name a single Whig except Fox, who was no historian, or a
single historian save Acton, who was no Whig.[2] But anything that the book lacked in detail and precision it made up
for in sparkling invective. The reader was left in no doubt
that the Whig interpretation was a bad thing ; and one of the
charges brought against it was that it 'studies the past with
reference to the present'. On this point Professor Butterfield
was categorical and severe :

> The study of the past with one eye, so to speak, upon
> the present is the source of all sins and sophistries in

[1] I am indebted here to Dr. W. Stark's excellent analysis of Meinecke's
development in his introduction to an English translation of *Die Idee der
Staatsräson*, published under the title *Machiavellism* in 1957; Dr. Stark
perhaps exaggerates the super-rational element in Meinecke's third period.

[2] H. Butterfield, *The Whig Interpretation of History* (1931) ; on p. 67
the author confesses to 'a healthy sort of distrust' of 'disembodied
reasoning'.

history. . . . It is the essence of what we mean by the word 'unhistorical'.[1]

Twelve years elapsed. The fashion for iconoclasm went out. Professor Butterfield's country was engaged in a war often said to be fought in defence of the constitutional liberties embodied in the Whig tradition, under a great leader who constantly invoked the past 'with one eye, so to speak, upon the present'. In a small book called *The Englishman and his History* published in 1944, Professor Butterfield not only decided that the Whig interpretation of history was the 'English' interpretation, but spoke enthusiastically of 'the Englishman's alliance with his history' and of the 'marriage between the present and the past'.[2] To draw attention to these reversals of outlook is not an unfriendly criticism. It is not my purpose to refute the proto-Butterfield with the deutero-Butterfield, or to confront Professor Butterfield drunk with Professor Butterfield sober. I am fully aware that, if anyone took the trouble to peruse some of the things I wrote before, during and after the war, he would have no difficulty at all in convicting me of contradictions and inconsistencies at least as glaring as any I have detected in others. Indeed, I am not sure that I should envy any historian who could honestly claim to have lived through the earth-shaking events of the past fifty years without some radical modifications of his outlook. My purpose is merely to show how closely the work of the historian mirrors the society in which he works. It is not merely the events that are in flux. The historian himself is in flux. When you take up an historical work, it is not enough to look for the author's name on the title-page : look also for the date of publication or writing — it is sometimes even more revealing. If the philosopher is right in telling us that we cannot step into the same river twice, it is perhaps equally

[1] H. Butterfield, *The Whig Interpretation of History* (1931), pp. 11, 31-32.
[2] H. Butterfield, *The Englishman and his History* (1944), pp. 2, 4-5.

true, and for the same reason, that two books cannot be written by the same historian.

And, if we move for a moment from the individual historian to what may be called broad trends in historical writing, the extent to which the historian is the product of his society becomes all the more apparent. In the nineteenth century British historians with scarcely an exception regarded the course of history as a demonstration of the principle of progress: they expressed the ideology of a society in a condition of remarkably rapid progress. History was full of meaning for British historians, so long as it seemed to be going our way; now that it has taken a wrong turning, belief in the meaning of history has become a heresy. After the first World War, Toynbee made a desperate attempt to replace a linear view of history by a cyclical theory — the characteristic ideology of a society in decline.[1] Since Toynbee's failure, British historians have for the most part been content to throw in their hands and declare that there is no general pattern in history at all. A banal remark by Fisher to that effect[2] has achieved almost as wide a popularity as Ranke's aphorism in the last century. If anyone tells me that the British historians of the last thirty years experienced this change of heart as the result of profound individual reflexion and of the burning of midnight oil in their separate garrets, I shall not think it necessary to contest the fact. But I shall continue to regard all this individual thinking and oil-burning as a social phenomenon, the product and expression of a fundamental change in the character and outlook of our society since 1914. There is no more significant pointer to the character of a society than the kind of history it writes or fails to write. Geyl, the Dutch historian, in his fascinating monograph translated into

[1] Marcus Aurelius in the twilight of the Roman Empire consoled himself by reflecting 'how all things that are now happening have happened in the past, and will happen in the future' (*To Himself*, x, 27); as is well known, Toynbee took the idea from Spengler's *Decline of the West*.

[2] Preface, dated December 4, 1934, to *A History of Europe*.

English under the title *Napoleon For and Against,* shows how the successive judgments of French nineteenth-century historians on Napoleon reflected the changing and conflicting patterns of French political life and thought throughout the century. The thought of historians, as of other human beings, is moulded by the environment of the time and place. Acton, who fully recognized this truth, sought for an escape from it in history itself:

> History [he wrote] must be our deliverer not only from the undue influence of other times, but from the undue influence of our own, from the tyranny of environment and the pressure of the air we breathe.[1]

This may sound too optimistic an assessment of the role of history. But I shall venture to believe that the historian who is most conscious of his own situation is also more capable of transcending it, and more capable of appreciating the essential nature of the differences between his own society and outlook and those of other periods and other countries, than the historian who loudly protests that he is an individual and not a social phenomenon. Man's capacity to rise above his social and historical situation seems to be conditioned by the sensitivity with which he recognizes the extent of his involvement in it.

In my first lecture I said : Before you study the history, study the historian. Now I would add : Before you study the historian, study his historical and social environment. The historian, being an individual, is also a product of history and of society ; and it is in this twofold light that the student of history must learn to regard him.

Let us now leave the historian and consider the other side of my equation — the facts of history — in the light of the same problem. Is the object of the historian's enquiry the behaviour of individuals or the action of social forces ? Here I am moving on to well-trodden ground. When Sir Isaiah

[1] Acton, *Lectures on Modern History* (1906), p. 33.

Berlin published a few years ago a sparkling and popular essay entitled *Historical Inevitability* — to the main thesis of which I shall return later in these lectures — he headed it with a motto culled from the works of Mr. T. S. Eliot 'Vast impersonal forces'; and throughout the essay he pokes fun at people who believe in 'vast impersonal forces' rather than individuals as the decisive factor in history. What I will call the Bad King John theory of history — the view that what matters in history is the character and behaviour of individuals — has a long pedigree. The desire to postulate individual genius as the creative force in history is characteristic of the primitive stages of historical consciousness. The ancient Greeks liked to label the achievements of the past with the names of eponymous heroes supposedly responsible for them, to attribute their epics to a bard called Homer, and their laws and institutions to a Lycurgus or a Solon. The same inclination reappears at the Renaissance when Plutarch, the biographer-moralist, was much more popular and influential a figure in the classical revival than the historians of antiquity, In this country, in particular, we all learned this theory, so to speak, at our mother's knee; and today we should probably recognize that there is something childish, or at any rate childlike, about it. It had some plausibility in days when society was simpler, and public affairs appeared to be run by a handful of known individuals. It clearly does not fit the more complex society of our times; and the birth in the nineteenth century of the new science of sociology was a response to this growing complexity. Yet the old tradition dies hard. At the beginning of this century, 'history is the biography of great men' was still a reputable dictum. Only ten years ago a distinguished American historian accused his colleagues, perhaps not too seriously, of the 'mass murder of historical characters' by treating them as 'puppets of social and economic forces'.[1] Addicts of this theory tend nowadays to be shy about it; but, after some searching, I found an excellent contemporary

[1] *American Historical Review*, lvi, No. 1 (January 1951), p. 270.

statement of it in the introduction to one of Miss Wedgwood's books.

> The behaviour of men as individuals [she writes] is more interesting to me than their behaviour as groups or classes. History can be written with this bias as well as another; it is neither more, nor less, misleading. . . . This book . . . is an attempt to understand how these men felt and why, in their own estimation, they acted as they did.[1]

This statement is precise; and, since Miss Wedgwood is a popular writer, many people, I am sure, think as she does. Dr. Rowse tells us, for instance, that the Elizabethan system broke down because James I was incapable of understanding it, and that the English revolution of the seventeenth century was an 'accidental' event due to the stupidity of the two first Stuart kings.[2] Even Sir James Neale, a more austere historian than Dr. Rowse, sometimes seems more eager to express his admiration for Queen Elizabeth than to explain what the Tudor monarchy stood for; and Sir Isaiah Berlin, in the essay which I have just quoted, is terribly worried by the prospect that historians may fail to denounce Genghis Khan and Hitler as bad men.[3] The Bad King John and Good Queen Bess theory is especially rife when we come to more recent times. It is easier to call communism 'the brain-child of Karl Marx' (I pluck this flower from a recent stockbrokers' circular) than to analyse its origin and character, to attribute the Bolshevik revolution to the stupidity of Nicholas II or to German gold than to study its profound social causes, and to see in the two world wars of this century the result of the individual wicked-

---

[1] C. V. Wedgwood, *The King's Peace* (1955), p. 17.
[2] A. L. Rowse, *The England of Elizabeth* (1950), pp. 261-262, 382. It is fair to point out that in an earlier essay Mr. Rowse condemned 'historians who think that the Bourbons failed to re-establish the monarchy in France after 1870 just because of Henry V's attachment to a little white flag' (*The End of an Epoch* (1949), p. 275); perhaps he reserves such personal explanations for English history.
[3] I. Berlin, *Historical Inevitability* (1954), p. 42.

ness of Wilheim II and Hitler rather than of some deep-seated breakdown in the system of international relations.

Miss Wedgwood's statement, then, combines two propositions. The first is that the behaviour of men as individuals is distinct from their behaviour as members of groups or classes, and that the historian may legitimately choose to dwell on the one rather than on the other. The second is that the study of the behaviour of men as individuals consists of the study of the conscious motives of their actions.

After what I have already said, I need not labour the first point. It is not that the view of man as an individual is more or less misleading than the view of him as a member of the group; it is the attempt to draw a distinction between the two which is misleading. The individual is by definition a member of a society, or probably of more than one society — call it group, class, tribe, nation or what you will. Early biologists were content to classify species of birds, beasts and fishes in cages, aquariums and showcases, and did not seek to study the living creature in relation to its environment. Perhaps the social sciences today have not yet fully emerged from that primitive stage. Some people distinguish between psychology as the science of the individual and sociology as the science of society; and the name 'psychologism' has been given to the view that all social problems are ultimately reducible to the analysis of individual human behaviour. But the psychologist who failed to study the social environment of the individual would not get very far.[1] It is tempting to make a distinction between biography which treats man as an individual and history which treats man as part of a whole,

[1] Modern psychologists have none the less been convicted of this error: 'Psychologists as a group have not treated the individual as a unit *in* a functioning social system, but rather as the concrete human being who was then conceived as proceeding to form social systems. They have thus not adequately taken account of the peculiar sense in which their categories are abstract' (Professor Talcott Parsons in the introduction to Max Weber, *The Theory of Social and Economic Organization* (1947), p. 27); see also the remarks on Freud, p. 133 below.

and to suggest that good biography makes bad history. 'Nothing causes more error and unfairness in man's view of history', Acton once wrote, 'than the interest which is inspired by individual characters.'[1] But this distinction, too, is unreal. Nor do I want to take shelter behind the Victorian proverb placed by G. M. Young on the title-page of his book *Victorian England*: 'Servants talk about people, gentlefolk discuss things'.[2] Some biographies are serious contributions to history : in my own field, Isaac Deutscher's biographies of Stalin and Trotsky are outstanding examples. Others belong to literature, like the historical novel. 'To Lytton Strachey', writes Professor Trevor-Roper, 'historical problems were always, and only, problems of individual behaviour and individual eccentricity. . . . Historical problems, the problems of politics and society, he never sought to answer, or even to ask.'[3] Nobody is obliged to write or read history ; and excellent books can be written about the past which are not history. But I think we are entitled by convention — as I propose to do in these lectures — to reserve the word 'history' for the process of enquiry into the past of man in society.

The second point, *i.e.* that history is concerned to enquire why individuals, 'in their own estimation, acted as they did', seems at first sight extremely odd ; and I suspect that Miss Wedgwood, like other sensible people, does not practise what she preaches. If she does, she must write some very queer history. Everyone knows today that human beings do not always, or perhaps even habitually, act from motives of which they are fully conscious or which they are willing to

[1] *Home and Foreign Review*, January 1863, p. 219.

[2] This idea was elaborated by Herbert Spencer in his most solemn style in *The Study of Sociology*, ch. 2 : 'If you want roughly to estimate anyone's mental calibre, you cannot do it better than by observing the ratio of generalities to personalities in his talk — how far simple truths about individuals are replaced by truths abstracted from numerous experiences of men and things. And when you have thus measured many, you find but a scattered few likely to take anything more than a biographical view of human affairs.'

[3] H. R. Trevor-Roper, *Historical Essays* (1957), p. 281.

avow ; and to exclude insight into unconscious or unavowed motives is surely a way of going about one's work with one eye wilfully shut. This is, however, what, according to some people, historians ought to do. The point is this. So long as you are content to say that the badness of King John consisted in his greed or stupidity or ambition to play the tyrant, you are speaking in terms of individual qualities which are comprehensible even at the level of nursery history. But, once you begin to say that King John was the unconscious tool of vested interests opposed to the rise to power of the feudal barons, you not only introduce a more complicated and sophisticated view of King John's badness, but you appear to suggest that historical events are determined not by the conscious actions of individuals, but by some extraneous and all-powerful forces guiding their unconscious will. This is, of course, nonsense. So far as I am concerned, I have no belief in Divine Providence, World Spirit, Manifest Destiny, History with a capital H, or any other of the abstractions which have sometimes been supposed to guide the course of events ; and I should endorse without qualification the comment of Marx :

> *History* does nothing, it possesses no immense wealth, fights no battles. It is rather *man*, real living *man* who does everything, who possesses and fights.[1]

The two remarks which I have to make on this question have nothing to do with any abstract view of history, and are based on purely empirical observation.

The first is that history is to a considerable extent a matter of numbers. Carlyle was responsible for the unfortunate assertion that 'history is the biography of great men'. But listen to him at his most eloquent and in his greatest historical work :

> Hunger and nakedness and righteous oppression lying heavy on 25 million hearts : this, not the wounded vanities or contradicted philosophies of philosophical

---

[1] *Marx-Engels : Gesamtausgabe*, I, iii, 625.

advocates, rich shopkeepers, rural noblesse, was the prime mover in the French revolution ; as the like will be in all such revolutions, in all countries.[1]

Or, as Lenin said, 'politics begin where the masses are, not where there are thousands, but where there are millions, that is where serious politics begin'.[2] Carlyle's and Lenin's millions were millions of individuals : there was nothing impersonal about them. Discussions of this question sometimes confuse anonymity with impersonality. People do not cease to be people, or individuals individuals, because we do not know their names. Mr. Eliot's 'vast, impersonal forces' were the individuals whom Clarendon, a bolder and franker conservative, calls 'dirty people of no name'.[3] These nameless millions were individuals acting, more or less unconsciously, together and constituting a social force. The historian will not in ordinary circumstances need to take cognizance of a single discontented peasant or discontented village. But millions of discontented peasants in thousands of villages are a factor which no historian will ignore. The reasons which deter Jones from getting married do not interest the historian unless the same reasons also deter thousands of other individuals of Jones's generation, and bring about a substantial fall in a marriage-rate : in that event, they may well be historically significant. Nor need we be perturbed by the platitude that movements are started by minorities. All effective movements have few leaders and a multitude of followers ; but this does not mean that the multitude is not essential to their success. Numbers count in history.

My second observation is even better attested. Writers of many different schools of thought have concurred in remarking that the actions of individual human beings . often

---

[1] *History of the French Revolution*, III, iii, ch. 1.
[2] Lenin, *Selected Works*, vii, 295.
[3] Clarendon, *A Brief View & Survey of the Dangerous & Pernicious Errors to Church & State in Mr. Hobbes' Book entitled Leviathan* (1676), p. 320.

have results which were not intended or desired by the actors or indeed by any other individual. The Christian believes that the individual, acting consciously for his own often selfish ends, is the unconscious agent of God's purpose. Mandeville's 'private vices — public benefits' was an early and deliberately paradoxical expression of this discovery. Adam Smith's hidden hand and Hegel's 'cunning of reason', which sets individuals to work for it and to serve its purposes, though the individuals believe themselves to be fulfilling their own personal desires, are too familiar to require quotation. 'In the social production of their means of production', wrote Marx in the preface to his *Critique of Political Economy*, 'human beings enter into definite and necessary relations which are independent of their will.' 'Man lives consciously for himself,' wrote Tolstoy in *War and Peace*, echoing Adam Smith, 'but is an unconscious instrument in the attainment of the historic, universal aims of humanity.'[1] And here, to round off this anthology, which is already long enough, is Professor Butterfield: 'There is something in the nature of historical events which twists the course of history in a direction that no man ever intended'.[2] Since 1914, after a hundred years of only minor local wars, we have had two major world wars. It would not be a plausible explanation of this phenomenon to maintain that more individuals wanted war, or fewer wanted peace, in the first half of the twentieth century than in the last three-quarters of the nineteenth. It is difficult to believe that any individual willed or desired the great economic depression of the 1930s. Yet it was indubitably brought about by the actions of individuals, each consciously pursuing some totally different aim. Nor does the diagnosis of a discrepancy between the intentions of the individual and the results of his action always have to wait for the retrospective historian. 'He does not mean to go to war,' wrote Lodge of Woodrow Wilson in March 1917,

[1] L. Tolstoy, *War and Peace*, ix, ch. 1.
[2] H. Butterfield, *The Englishman and His History* (1944), p. 103.

'but I think he will be carried away by events.'[1] It defies all the evidence to suggest that history can be written on the basis of 'explanations in terms of human intentions'[2] or of accounts of their motives given by the actors themselves, of why, 'in their own estimation, they acted as they did'. The facts of history are indeed facts about individuals, but not about actions of individuals performed in isolation, and not about the motives, real or imaginary, from which individuals suppose themselves to have acted. They are facts about the relations of individuals to one another in society and about the social forces which produce from the actions of individuals results often at variance with, and sometimes opposite to, the results which they themselves intended.

One of the serious errors of Collingwood's view of history which I discussed in my last lecture was to assume that the thought behind the act, which the historian was called on to investigate, was the thought of the individual actor. This is a false assumption. What the historian is called on to investigate is what lies behind the act; and to this the conscious thought or motive of the individual actor may be quite irrelevant.

Here I should say something about the role of the rebel or dissident in history. To set up the popular picture of the individual in revolt against society is to re-introduce the false antithesis between society and the individual. No society is fully homogeneous. Every society is an arena of social conflicts, and those individuals who range themselves against existing authority are no less products and reflexions of the society than those who uphold it. Richard II and Catherine the Great represented powerful social forces in the England of the fourteenth century and in the Russia of the eighteenth century: but so also did Wat Tyler and Pugachev, the leader

---

[1] Quoted in B. W. Tuchman, *The Zimmermann Telegram* (N.Y., 1958), p. 180.

[2] The phrase is quoted from I. Berlin, *Historical Inevitability* (1954), p. 7, where the writing of history in these terms appears to be commended.

of the great serf rebellion. Monarchs and rebels alike were the product of the specific conditions of their age and country. To describe Wat Tyler and Pugachev as individuals in revolt against society is a misleading simplification. If they had been merely that, the historian would never have heard of them. They owe their role in history to the mass of their followers, and are significant as social phenomena, or not at all. Or let us take an outstanding rebel and individualist at a more sophisticated level. Few people have reacted more violently and more radically against the society of their day and country than Nietzsche. Yet Nietzsche was a direct product of European, and more specifically of German, society — a phenomenon which could not have occurred in China or Peru. A generation after Nietzsche's death it became clearer than it had been to his contemporaries how strong were the European, and specifically German, social forces of which this individual had been the expression; and Nietzsche became a more significant figure for posterity than for his own generation.

The role of the rebel in history has some analogies with that of the great man. The great man theory of history — a particular example of the Good Queen Bess school — has gone out of fashion in recent years, though it still occasionally rears its ungainly head. The editor of a series of popular history text-books started after the second World War invited his authors 'to open up a significant historical theme by way of a biography of a great man'; and Mr. A. J. P. Taylor told us in one of his minor essays that 'the history of modern Europe can be written in terms of three titans: Napoleon, Bismarck and Lenin',[1] though in his more serious writings he has undertaken no such rash project. What is the role of the great man in history? The great man is an individual, and, being an outstanding individual, is also a social phenomenon of outstanding importance. 'It is an obvious truth', observed Gibbon, 'that the times must be suited to extraordinary characters, and that the genius of Cromwell or Retz might

[1] A. J. P. Taylor, *From Napoleon to Stalin* (1950), p. 74.

now expire in obscurity.'[1] Marx in *The Eighteenth Brumaire of Louis Bonaparte* diagnosed the converse phenomenon: 'The class war in France created circumstances and relations which enabled a gross mediocrity to strut about in a hero's garb'. Had Bismarck been born in the eighteenth century — an absurd hypothesis, since he would not then have been Bismarck — he would not have united Germany, and might not have been a great man at all. But one need not, I think, as Tolstoy does, decry great men as no more than 'labels giving names to events'. Sometimes of course the cult of the great man may have sinister implications. Nietzsche's superman is a repellent figure. It is not necessary for me to recall the case of Hitler, or the grim consequences of the 'cult of personality' in the Soviet Union. But it is not my purpose to deflate the greatness of great men: nor do I want to subscribe to the thesis that 'great men are almost always bad men'. The view which I would hope to discourage is the view which places great men outside history and sees them as imposing themselves on history in virtue of their greatness, as 'jack-in-the-boxes who emerge miraculously from the unknown to interrupt the real continuity of history'.[2] Even today I do not know that we can better Hegel's classic description:

> The great man of the age is the one who can put into words the will of his age, tell his age what its will is, and accomplish it. What he does is the heart and essence of his age; he actualises his age.[3]

Dr. Leavis means something like this when he says that great writers are 'significant in terms of the human awareness they promote'.[4] The great man is always representative either of existing forces or of forces which he helps to create by way of

---

[1] Gibbon, *Decline and Fall of the Roman Empire*, ch. lxx.
[2] V. G. Childe, *History* (1947), p. 43.
[3] *Philosophy of Right* (English transl., 1942), p. 295.
[4] F. R. Leavis, *The Great Tradition* (1948), p. 2.

challenge to existing authority. But the higher degree of creativity may perhaps be assigned to those great men who, like Cromwell or Lenin, helped to mould the forces which carried them to greatness, rather than to those who, like Napoleon or Bismarck, rode to greatness on the back of already existing forces. Nor should we forget those great men who stood so far in advance of their own time that their greatness was recognized only by succeeding generations. What seems to me essential is to recognize in the great man an outstanding individual who is at once a product and an agent of the historical process, at once the representative and the creator of social forces which change the shape of the world and the thoughts of men.

History, then, in both senses of the word — meaning both the enquiry conducted by the historian and the facts of the past into which he enquires — is a social process, in which individuals are engaged as social beings; and the imaginary antithesis between society and the individual is no more than a red herring drawn across our path to confuse our thinking. The reciprocal process of interaction between the historian and his facts, what I have called the dialogue between present and past, is a dialogue not between abstract and isolated individuals, but between the society of today and the society of yesterday. History, in Burckhardt's words, is 'the record of what one age finds worthy of note in another'.[1] The past is intelligible to us only in the light of the present; and we can fully understand the present only in the light of the past. To enable man to understand the society of the past and to increase his mastery over the society of the present is the dual function of history.

[1] J. Burckhardt, *Judgements on History and on Historians* (1959) p. 158.

## III

# *History, Science and Morality*

WHEN I was very young, I was suitably impressed to learn that, appearances notwithstanding, the whale is not a fish. Nowadays these questions of classification move me less; and it does not worry me unduly when I am assured that history is not a science. This terminological question is an eccentricity of the English language. In every other European language, the equivalent word to 'science' includes history without hesitation. But in the English-speaking world this question has a long past behind it, and the issues raised by it are a convenient introduction to the problems of method in history.

At the end of the eighteenth century, when science had contributed so triumphantly both to man's knowledge of the world and to man's knowledge of his own physical attributes, it began to be asked whether science could not also further man's knowledge of society. The conception of the social sciences, and of history among them, gradually developed throughout the nineteenth century; and the method by which science studied the world of nature was applied to the study of human affairs. In the first part of this period the Newtonian tradition prevailed. Society, like the world of nature, was thought of as a mechanism; the title of a work by Herbert Spencer, *Social Statics*, published in 1851, is still remembered. Bertrand Russell, reared in this tradition, later recalled the period when he hoped that in time there would be 'a mathematics of human behaviour as precise as the mathematics of machines'.[1] Then Darwin made another

[1] B. Russell, *Portraits from Memory* (1958), p. 20.

50

scientific revolution; and social scientists, taking their cue from biology, began to think of society as an organism. But the real importance of the Darwinian revolution was that Darwin, completing what Lyell had already begun in geology, brought history into science. Science was concerned no longer with something static and timeless,[1] but with a process of change and development. Evolution in science confirmed and complemented progress in history. Nothing, however, occurred to alter the inductive view of historical method which I described in my first lecture : first collect your facts, then interpret them. It was assumed without question that this was also the method of science. This was the view which Bury evidently had in mind when, in the closing words of his inaugural lecture of January 1903, he described history as 'a science, no more and no less'. The fifty years after Bury's inaugural witnessed a strong reaction against this view of history. Collingwood, when he wrote in the 1930s, was particularly anxious to draw a sharp line between the world of nature, which was the object of scientific enquiry, and the world of history ; and during this period Bury's dictum was rarely quoted except in terms of derision. But what historians failed to notice at the time was that science itself had undergone a profound revolution, which makes it seem that Bury may have been more nearly right than we had supposed, though for the wrong reason. What Lyell did for geology and Darwin for biology has now been done for astronomy, which has become a science of how the universe came to be what it is ; and modern physicists constantly tell us that what they investigate are not facts, but events. The historian has some excuse for feeling himself more at home in the world of science today than he could have done a hundred years ago.

Let us look first at the concept of laws. Throughout the eighteenth and nineteenth centuries, scientists assumed that

[1] As late as 1874, Bradley distinguished science from history as being concerned with the timeless and 'abiding' (F. H. Bradley, *Collected Essays* (1935), i, 36).

laws of nature — Newton's laws of motion, the law of gravitation, Boyle's law, the law of evolution, and so forth — had been discovered and definitely established, and that the business of the scientist was to discover and establish more such laws by process of induction from observed facts. The word 'law' came down trailing clouds of glory from Galileo and Newton. Students of society, consciously or unconsciously desiring to assert the scientific status of their studies, adopted the same language and believed themselves to be following the same procedure. The political economists seem to have been first in the field with Gresham's law, and Adam Smith's laws of the market. Burke appealed to 'the laws of commerce, which are the laws of nature, and consequently the Laws of God'.[1] Malthus propounded a law of population; Lassalle an iron law of wages; and Marx in the preface to *Capital* claimed to have discovered 'the economic law of motion of modern society'. Buckle in the concluding words of his *History of Civilization* expressed the conviction that the course of human affairs was 'permeated by one glorious principle of universal and undeviating regularity'. Today this terminology sounds as old-fashioned as it is presumptuous; but it sounds almost as old-fashioned to the physical scientist as it does to the social scientist. In the year before Bury delivered his inaugural lecture, the French mathematician Henri Poincaré published a small volume called *La Science et l'hypothèse* which started a revolution in scientific thinking. Poincaré's main thesis was that the general propositions enunciated by scientists, where they were not mere definitions or disguised conventions about the use of language, were hypotheses designed to crystallize and organize further thinking, and were subject to verification, modification or refutation. All this has now become something of a commonplace. Newton's boast 'Hypotheses non

[1] *Thoughts and Details on Scarcity* (1795) in *The Works of Edmund Burke* (1846), iv, 270; Burke deduced that it was not 'within the competence of the government, taken as government, or even of the rich, as rich, to supply to the poor those necessaries which it has pleased the Divine Providence for awhile to withhold from them'.

fingo' rings hollow today; and though scientists, and even social scientists, still sometimes speak of laws, so to speak, for old time's sake, they no longer believe in their existence in the sense in which scientists of the eighteenth and nineteenth century universally believed in them. It is recognized that scientists make discoveries and acquire fresh knowledge, not by establishing precise and comprehensive laws, but by enunciating hypotheses which open the way to fresh enquiry. A standard text-book on scientific method by two American philosophers describes the method of science as 'essentially circular':

> We obtain evidence for principles by appealing to empirical material, to what is alleged to be 'fact'; and we select, analyse and interpret empirical material on the basis of principles.[1]

The word 'reciprocal' would perhaps have been preferable to 'circular'; for the result is not to return to the same place, but to move forward to fresh discoveries through this process of interaction between principles and facts, between theory and practice. All thinking requires acceptance of certain presuppositions based on observation which make scientific thinking possible, but are subject to revision in the light of that thinking. These hypotheses may well be valid in some contexts or for some purposes, though they turn out to be invalid in others. The test in all cases is the empirical one whether they are in fact effective in promoting fresh insights and adding to our knowledge. The methods of Rutherford were recently described by one of his most distinguished pupils and fellow-workers:

> He had a driving urge to know how nuclear phenomena worked in the sense in which one could speak of knowing what went on in the kitchen. I do not believe that he searched for an explanation in the classical manner of a

[1] M. R. Cohen and E. Nagel, *Introduction to Logic and Scientific Method* (1934), p. 596.

theory using certain basic laws ; as long as he knew what was happening he was content.[1]

This description equally fits the historian, who has abandoned the search for basic laws, and is content to enquire how things work.

The status of the hypotheses used by the historian in the process of his enquiry seems remarkably similar to that of the hypotheses used by the scientist. Take, for example, Max Weber's famous diagnosis of a relation between Protestantism and capitalism. Nobody today would call this a law, though it might have been hailed as such in an earlier period. It is a hypothesis which, though modified to some extent in the course of the enquiries which it inspired, has beyond doubt enlarged our understanding of both these movements. Or take a statement like that of Marx : 'The hand-mill gives us a society with a feudal lord ; the steam-mill gives us a society with an industrial capitalist'.[2] This is not in modern terminology a law, though Marx would probably have claimed it as such, but a fruitful hypothesis pointing the way to further enquiry and fresh understanding. Such hypotheses are indispensable tools of thought. The well-known German economist of the early 1900s, Werner Sombart, confessed to a 'troubled feeling' which overtook those who had abandoned Marxism.

> When [he wrote] we lose the comfortable formulas that have hitherto been our guides amid the complexities of existence . . . we feel like drowning in the ocean of facts until we find a new foothold or learn to swim.[3]

The controversy about periodization in history falls into this category. The division of history into periods is not a fact, but a necessary hypothesis or tool of thought, valid in so far

[1] Sir Charles Ellis in *Trinity Review* (Cambridge, Lent Term, 1960), p. 14.
[2] *Marx-Engels: Gesamtausgabe*, I, vi, 179.
[3] W. Sombart, *The Quintessence of Capitalism* (Engl. transl., 1915), p. 354.

as it is illuminating, and dependent for its validity on interpretation. Historians who differ on the question when the
Middle Ages ended differ in their interpretation of certain
events. The question is not a question of fact; but it is also
not meaningless. The division of history into geographical
sectors is equally not a fact, but a hypothesis: to speak of
European history may be a valid and fruitful hypothesis in
some contexts, misleading and mischievous in others. Most
historians assume that Russia is part of Europe; some pas-
sionately deny it. The bias of the historian can be judged by
the hypothesis which he adopts. I must quote one general
pronouncement on the methods of social science, since it
comes from a great social scientist who was trained as a
physical scientist. Georges Sorel, who practised as an engineer
before he began in his forties to write about the problems of
society, emphasized the need to isolate particular elements in
a situation even at the risk of over-simplifying:

> One should proceed [he wrote] by feeling one's way;
> one should try out probable and partial hypotheses, and
> be satisfied with provisional approximations so as always
> to leave the door open to progressive correction.[1]

This is a far cry from the nineteenth century, when scientists,
and historians like Acton, looked forward to one day establishing, through the accumulation of well-attested facts, a comprehensive body of knowledge which would settle all disputed
issues once for all. Nowadays both scientists and historians
entertain the more modest hope of advancing progressively
from one fragmentary hypothesis to another, isolating their
facts through the medium of their interpretations, and testing
their interpretations by the facts; and ways in which they go
about it do not seem to me essentially different. In my first
lecture I quoted a remark of Professor Barraclough that history was 'not factual at all, but a series of accepted judgments'.
While I was preparing these lectures, a physicist from this

[1] G. Sorel, *Matériaux d'une théorie du prolétariat* (1919), p. 7.

university, in a B.B.C. broadcast, defined a scientific truth as 'a statement which has been publicly accepted by the experts'.[1] Neither of these formulas is entirely satisfactory — for reasons which will appear when I come to discuss the question of objectivity. But it was striking to find a historian and a physicist independently formulating the same problem in almost exactly the same words.

Analogies are, however, a notorious trap for the unwary : and I want to consider respectfully the arguments for believing that, great as are the differences between the mathematical and the natural sciences, or between different sciences within these categories, a fundamental distinction can be drawn between these sciences and history, and that this distinction makes it misleading to call history — and perhaps also the other so-called social sciences — by the name of science. These objections — some of them more convincing than others — are in brief : (1) that history deals exclusively with the unique, science with the general, (2) that history teaches no lessons, (3) that history is unable to predict, (4) that history is necessarily subjective, since man is observing himself, and (5) that history, unlike science, involves issues of religion and morality. I will try to examine each of these points in turn.


First, it is alleged that history deals with the unique and particular, and science with the general and universal. This view may be said to start with Aristotle, who declared that poetry was 'more philosophical' and 'more serious' than history, since poetry was concerned with general truth and history with particular.[2] A host of later writers, down to Collingwood[3] inclusive, made a similar distinction between science and history. This seems to rest on a misunderstanding. Hobbes's famous dictum still stands : 'Nothing in the world

[1] Dr. J. Ziman in *The Listener*, August 18, 1960.
[2] *Poetics*, ch. ix.
[3] R. G. Collingwood, *Historical Imagination* (1935), p. 5.

is universal but names, for the things named are everyone of them individual and singular'.[1] This is certainly true of the physical sciences: no two geological formations, no two animals of the same species, and no two atoms, are identical. Similarly, no two historical events are identical. But insistence on the uniqueness of historical events has the same paralysing effect as the platitude taken over by Moore from Bishop Butler and at one time especially beloved by linguistic philosophers: 'Everything is what it is and not another thing'. Embarked on this course, you soon attain a sort of philosophical *nirvana*, in which nothing that matters can be said about anything.

The very use of language commits the historian, like the scientist, to generalization. The Peloponnesian War and the second World War were very different, and both were unique. But the historian calls them both wars, and only the pedant will protest. When Gibbon wrote of both the establishment of Christianity by Constantine and the rise of Islam as revolutions,[2] he was generalizing two unique events. Modern historians do the same when they write of the English, French, Russian and Chinese revolutions. The historian is not really interested in the unique, but in what is general in the unique. In the 1920s discussions by historians of the causes of the war of 1914 usually proceeded on the assumption that it was due either to the mismanagement of diplomats, working in secret and uncontrolled by public opinion, or to the unfortunate division of the world into territorial sovereign states. In the 1930s discussions proceeded on the assumption that it was due to rivalries between imperialist Powers driven by the stresses of capitalism in decline to partition the world between them. These discussions all involved generalization about the causes of war, or at any rate of war in twentieth-century conditions. The historian constantly uses generalization to test his evidence. If the evidence is not clear whether Richard

[1] *Leviathan*, I, iv.
[2] *Decline and Fall of the Roman Empire*, ch. xx, ch. l.

murdered the princes in the Tower, the historian will ask himself — perhaps unconsciously rather than consciously — whether it was a habit of rulers of the period to liquidate potential rivals to their throne; and his judgment will, quite rightly, be influenced by this generalization.

The reader, as well as the writer, of history, is a chronic generalizer, applying the observation of the historian to other historical contexts with which he is familiar — or perhaps to his own time. When I read Carlyle's *French Revolution*, I find myself again and again generalizing his comments by applying them to my own special interest in the Russian revolution. Take for instance this on the terror:

> Horrible, in lands that had known equal justice — not so unnatural in lands that had never known it.

Or, more significantly, this:

> It is unfortunate, though very natural, that the history of this period has so generally been written in hysterics. Exaggeration abounds, execration, wailing; and on the whole, darkness.[1]

Or another, this time from Burckhardt on the growth of the modern state in the sixteenth century:

> The more recently power has originated, the less it can remain stationary — first because those who created it have become accustomed to rapid further movement and because they are and will remain innovators *per se*; secondly, because the forces aroused or subdued by them can be employed only through further acts of violence.[2]

It is nonsense to say that generalization is foreign to history; history thrives on generalizations. As Mr. Elton neatly puts it in a volume of the new *Cambridge Modern History*, 'what distinguishes the historian from the collector of historical facts is generalization';[3] he might have added that the same

[1] *History of the French Revolution*, I, v, ch. 9; III, i, ch. 1.
[2] J. Burckhardt, *Judgements on History and Historians* (1959), p. 34.
[3] *Cambridge Modern History*, ii (1958), 20.

thing distinguishes the natural scientist from the naturalist or collector of specimens. But do not suppose that generalization permits us to construct some vast scheme of history into which specific events must be fitted. And, since Marx is one of those who is often accused of constructing, or believing in, such a scheme, I will quote by way of summing-up a passage from one of his letters which puts the matter in its right perspective :

> Events strikingly similar, but occurring in a different historical milieu, lead to completely dissimilar results. By studying each of these evolutions separately and then comparing them, it is easy to find the key to the understanding of this phenomenon ; but it is never possible to arrive at this understanding by using the *passe-partout* of some historical-philosophical theory whose great virtue is to stand above history.[1]

History is concerned with the relation between the unique and the general. As a historian, you can no more separate them, or give precedence to one over the other, than you can separate fact and interpretation.

This is perhaps the place for a brief remark on the relations between history and sociology. Sociology at present faces two opposite dangers — the danger of becoming ultra-theoretical and the danger of becoming ultra-empirical. The first is the danger of losing itself in abstract and meaningless generalizations about society in general. Society with a big S is as misleading a fallacy as History with a big H. This danger is brought nearer by those who assign to sociology the exclusive task of generalizing from the unique events recorded by history : it has even been suggested that sociology

---

[1] Marx and Engels, *Works* (Russian ed.), xv, 378 ; the letter from which this passage is quoted appeared in the Russian journal *Otechest-vennye Zapiski* in 1877. Professor Popper appears to associate Marx with what he calls 'the central mistake of historicism', the belief that historical tendencies or trends 'can be immediately derived from universal laws alone' (*The Poverty of Historicism* (1957), pp. 128-129) : this is precisely what Marx denied.

is distinguished from history by having 'laws'.[1] The other danger is that foreseen by Karl Mannheim almost a generation ago, and very much present today, of a sociology 'split into a series of discrete technical problems of social readjustment'.[2] Sociology is concerned with historical societies every one of which is unique and moulded by specific historical antecedents and conditions. But the attempt to avoid generalization and interpretation by confining oneself to so-called 'technical' problems of enumeration and analysis is merely to become the unconscious apologist of a static society. Sociology, if it is to become a fruitful field of study, must, like history, concern itself with the relation between the unique and the general. But it must also become dynamic — a study not of society at rest (for no such society exists), but of social change and development. For the rest, I would only say that the more sociological history becomes, and the more historical sociology becomes, the better for both. Let the frontier between them be kept wide open for two-way traffic.

The question of generalization is closely connected with my second question : the lessons of history. The real point about generalization is that through it we attempt to learn from history, to apply the lesson drawn from one set of events to another set of events : when we generalize, we are consciously or unconsciously trying to do this. Those who reject generalization and insist that history is concerned exclusively

[1] This appears to be the view of Professor Popper (*The Open Society* (2nd ed., 1952), ii, 322). Unfortunately he gives an example of a sociological law : 'Wherever the freedom of thought, and of the communication of thought, is effectively protected by legal institutions and institutions ensuring the publicity of discussion, there will be scientific progress'. This was written in 1942 or 1943, and was evidently inspired by the belief that the western democracies, in virtue of their institutional arrangements, would remain in the van of scientific progress — a belief since dispelled, or severely qualified, by developments in the Soviet Union. Far from being a law, it was not even a valid generalization.

[2] K. Mannheim, *Ideology and Utopia* (Engl. trans., 1936), p. 228.

with the unique are, logically enough, those who deny that anything can be learned from history. But the assertion that men learn nothing from history is contradicted by a multitude of observable facts. No experience is more common. In 1919 I was present at the Paris peace conference as a junior member of the British delegation. Everyone in the delegation believed that we could learn from the lessons of the Vienna congress, the last great European peace congress a hundred years earlier. A certain Captain Webster, then employed in the War Office, now Sir Charles Webster and an eminent historian, wrote an essay telling us what those lessons were. Two of them have remained in my memory. One was that it was dangerous, when re-drawing the map of Europe, to neglect the principle of self-determination. The other was that it was dangerous to throw secret documents into your waste-paper basket, the contents of which would certainly be bought by the secret service of some other delegation. These lessons of history were taken for gospel and influenced our behaviour. This example is recent and trivial. But it would be easy to trace in comparatively remote history the influence of the lessons of a still remoter past. Everyone knows about the impact of ancient Greece upon Rome. But I am not sure whether any historian has attempted to make a precise analysis of the lessons which the Romans learned, or believed themselves to have learned, from the history of Hellas. An examination of the lessons drawn in western Europe in the seventeenth, eighteenth and nineteenth centuries from Old Testament history might yield rewarding results. The English Puritan revolution cannot be fully understood without it; and the conception of the chosen people was an important factor in the rise of modern nationalism. The stamp of a classical education was heavily imprinted in the nineteenth century on the new ruling class in Great Britain. Grote, as I have already noted, pointed to Athens as an exemplar for the new democracy; and I should like to see a study of the extensive and important lessons consciously or unconsciously imparted to British empire-builders by the history of the Roman Empire. In my own particular field, the makers of the Russian revolution were profoundly impressed — one might almost say, obsessed — by the lessons of the French revolution, of the revolutions of 1848 and of the Paris commune of 1871. But I shall recall here the qualification imposed by the dual character of history. Learning from history is never simply a one-way process. . To learn about the present in the light of the past means also to learn about the past in the light of the present. The function of history is to promote a profounder understanding of both past and present through the interrelation between them.

My third point is the role of prediction in history : no lessons, it is said, can be learned from history because history, unlike science, cannot predict the future. This question is involved in a tissue of misunderstandings. As we have seen, scientists are no longer so eager as they used to be to talk about the laws of nature. The so-called laws of sciences which affect our ordinary life are in fact statements of tendency, statements of what will happen other things being equal or in laboratory conditions. They do not claim to predict what will happen in concrete cases. The law of gravity does not prove that that particular apple will fall to the ground : somebody may catch it in a basket. The law of optics that light travels in a straight line does not prove that a particular ray of light may not be refracted or scattered by some intervening object. But this does not mean that these laws are worthless, or not in principle valid. Modern physical theories, we are told, deal only with the probabilities of events taking place. Today science is more inclined to remember that induction can logically lead only to probabilities or to reasonable belief, and is more anxious to treat its pronouncements as general rules or guides, the validity of which can be tested only in specific action. 'Science, d'où prévoyance ;

prévoyance, d'où action', as Comte put it.'[1] The clue to the question of prediction in history lies in this distinction between the general and the specific, between the universal and the unique. The historian, as we have seen, is bound to generalize; and, in so doing, he provides general guides for future action which, though not specific predictions, are both valid and useful. But he cannot predict specific events, because the specific is unique and because the element of accident enters into it. This distinction, which worries philosophers, is perfectly clear to the ordinary man. If two or three children in a school develop measles, you will conclude that the epidemic will spread; and this prediction, if you care to call it such, is based on a generalization from past experience, and is a valid and useful guide to action. But you cannot make the specific prediction that Charles or Mary will catch measles. The historian proceeds in the same way. People do not expect the historian to predict that revolution will break out in Ruritania next month. The kind of conclusion which they will seek to draw, partly from specific knowledge of Ruritanian affairs and partly from a study of history, is that conditions in Ruritania are such that a revolution is likely to occur in the near future if somebody touches it off, or unless somebody on the government side does something to stop it; and this conclusion might be accompanied by estimates, based partly on the analogy of other revolutions, of the attitude which different sectors of the population may be expected to adopt. The prediction, if such it can be called, can be realized only through the occurrence of unique events, which cannot themselves be predicted. But this does not mean that inferences drawn from history about the future are worthless, or that they do not possess a conditional validity which serves both as a guide to action and a key to our understanding of how things happen. I do not wish to suggest that the inferences of the social scientist or of the historian can match those of the physical scientist in precision, or that their inferiority

[1] *Cours de philosophie positive*, i, 51.

in this respect is due merely to the greater backwardness of the social sciences. The human being is on any view the most complex natural entity known to us, and the study of his behaviour may well involve difficulties different in kind from those confronting the physical scientist. All I wish to establish is that their aims and methods are not fundamentally dissimilar.

My fourth point introduces a far more cogent argument for drawing a line of demarcation between the social sciences, including history, and the physical sciences. This is the argument that in the social sciences subject and object belong to the same category and interact reciprocally on each other. Human beings are not only the most complex and variable of natural entities, but they have to be studied by other human beings, not by independent observers of another species. Here man is no longer content, as in the biological sciences, to study his own physical make-up and physical reactions. The sociologist, the economist or the historian needs to penetrate into forms of human behaviour in which the will is active, to ascertain why the human beings who are the object of his study willed to act as they did. This sets up a relation which is peculiar to history and the social sciences between the observer and what is observed. The point of view of the historian enters irrevocably into every observation which he makes ; history is shot through and through with relativity. In Karl Mannheim's words, 'even the categories in which experiences are subsumed, collected and ordered vary according to the social position of the observer'.[1] But it is not merely true that the bias of the social scientist necessarily enters into all his observations. It is also true that the process of observation affects and modifies what is being observed. And this can happen in two opposite ways. The human beings whose behaviour is made the object of analysis and prediction

[1] K. Mannheim, *Ideology and Utopia* (1936), p. 130.

may be warned in advance by the prediction of consequences unwelcome to them, and be induced by it to modify their action, so that the prediction, however correctly based on the analysis, proves self-frustrating. One reason why history rarely repeats itself among historically conscious people is that the *dramatis personae* are aware at the second performance of the *dénouement* of the first, and their action is affected by that knowledge.[1] The Bolsheviks knew that the French revolution had ended in a Napoleon, and feared that their own revolution might end in the same way. They therefore mistrusted Trotsky, who among their leaders looked most like a Napoleon, and trusted Stalin, who looked least like a Napoleon. But this process may work in a converse direction. The economist who, by a scientific analysis of existing economic conditions, predicts an approaching boom or slump may, if his authority is great and his arguments cogent, contribute by the very fact of his prediction to the occurrence of the phenomenon predicted. The political scientist who, on the strength of historical observations, nourishes the conviction that despotism is short-lived, may contribute to the downfall of the despot. Everyone is familiar with the behaviour of candidates at elections who predict their own victory for the conscious purpose of rendering the fulfilment of the prediction more likely; and one suspects that economists, political scientists and historians, when they venture on prediction, are sometimes inspired by the unconscious hope of hastening the realization of the prediction. All that one can perhaps safely say about these complex relations is that interaction between the observer and what is observed, between the social scientist and his data, between the historian and his facts, is continuous, and continuously varies; and that this appears to be a distinctive feature of history and of the social sciences.

I should perhaps note here that some physicists in recent years have spoken of their science in terms which appear to

[1] This argument has been developed by the author in *The Bolshevik Revolution, 1917–1923*, i (1950), 42.

suggest more striking analogies between the physical universe and the world of the historian. In the first place, their results are said to involve a principle of uncertainty or indeterminacy. I shall speak in my next lecture of the nature and limits of so-called determinism in history. But whether the indeterminacy of modern physics resides in the nature of the universe or is merely an index of our own hitherto imperfect understanding of it (this point is still in debate), I should have the same doubts about finding in it significant analogies with our ability to make historical predictions as one had a few years ago about the attempts of some enthusiasts to find proof in it of the operation of free will in the universe. Secondly, we are told that in modern physics distances in space and lapses of time have measures depending on the motion of the 'observer'. In modern physics all measurements are subject to inherent variations due to the impossibility of establishing a constant relation between the 'observer' and the object under observation ; both the 'observer' and the thing observed — both subject and object — enter into the final result of the observation. But, while these descriptions would apply with a minimum of change to the relations between the historian and the objects of his observations, I am not satisfied that the essence of these relations is in any real sense comparable with the nature of relations between the physicist and his universe ; and though I am in principle concerned to reduce rather than to inflate the differences which separate the approach of the historian from that of the scientist, it will not help to attempt to spirit these differences away by relying on imperfect analogies.

But, while it is, I think, fair to say that the involvement of the social scientist or historian in the object of his study is of a different kind from that of the physical scientist, and the issues raised by the relation between subject and object infinitely more complicated, this is not the end of the matter. Classical theories of knowledge, which prevailed throughout the seventeenth, eighteenth and nineteenth centuries, all assumed a sharp dichotomy between the knowing subject and the object known. However the process was conceived, the model constructed by the philosophers showed subject and object, man and the external world, divided and apart. This was the great age of the birth and development of science ; and theories of knowledge were strongly influenced by the outlook of the pioneers of science. Man was set sharply against the external world. He grappled with it as with something intractable and potentially hostile — intractable because it was difficult to understand, potentially hostile because it was difficult to master. With the successes of modern science, this outlook has been radically modified. The scientist nowadays is far less likely to think of the forces of nature as something to fight against than as something to cooperate with and to harness to his purposes. Classical theories of knowledge no longer fit the newer science, and least of all the science of physics. It is not surprising that during the past fifty years philosophers have begun to call them in question, and to recognize that the process of knowledge, far from setting subject and object sharply apart, involves a measure of interrelation and interdependence between them. This is, however, extremely significant for the social sciences. In my first lecture, I suggested that the study of history was difficult to reconcile with the traditional empiricist theory of knowledge. I should now like to argue that the social sciences as a whole, since they involve man as both subject and object, both investigator and thing investigated, are incompatible with any theory of knowledge which pronounces a rigid divorce between subject and object. Sociology, in its attempts to establish itself as a coherent body of doctrine, has quite rightly set up a branch called the sociology of knowledge. This has, however, not yet got very far — mainly, I suspect, because it has been content to go round and round inside the cage of a traditional theory of knowledge. If philosophers, under the impact first of modern physical science, and now of modern social science, are beginning to break out from this cage, and construct some more up-to-date model for the processes of knowledge than the old billiard-ball model of the impact of data on a passive consciousness, this is a good omen for the social sciences and for history in particular. This is a point of some importance to which I shall return later when I come to consider what we mean by objectivity in history.

Last but not least, I have to discuss the view that history, being intimately involved in questions of religion and morality, is thereby distinguished from science in general, and perhaps even from the other social sciences. Of the relation of history to religion I shall say only the little that is necessary to make my own position clear. To be a serious astronomer is compatible with belief in a God who created and ordered the universe. But it is not compatible with belief in a God who intervenes at will to change the course of a planet, to postpone an eclipse, or to alter the rules of the cosmic game. In the same way, it is sometimes suggested, a serious historian may believe in a God who has ordered, and given meaning to, the course of history as a whole, though he cannot believe in the Old Testament kind of God who intervenes to slaughter the Amalekites, or cheats on the calendar by extending the hours of daylight for the benefit of Joshua's army. Nor can he invoke God as an explanation of particular historical events. Father D'Arcy in a recent book attempted to make this distinction :

> It would not do for a student to answer every question in history by saying that it was the finger of God. Not until we have gone as far as most in tidying up mundane events and the human drama are we permitted to bring in wider considerations.[1]

[1] M. C. D'Arcy, *The Sense of History : Secular and Sacred* (1959), p. 164; he had been anticipated by Polybius : 'Wherever it is possible to find out the cause of what is happening one should not have recourse to the gods' (quoted in K. von Fritz, *The Theory of the Mixed Constitution in Antiquity* (N.Y., 1954), p. 390).

The awkwardness of this view is that it appears to treat religion like the joker in the pack of cards, to be reserved for really important tricks that cannot be taken in any other way. Karl Barth, the Lutheran theologian, did better when he pronounced a total separation between divine and secular history, and handed over the latter to the secular arm. Professor Butterfield, if I understand him, means the same thing when he speaks of 'technical' history. Technical history is the only kind of history you or I are ever likely to write, or he himself has ever written. But by the use of this odd epithet, he reserves the right to believe in an esoteric or providential history with which the rest of us need not concern ourselves. Writers like Berdyaev, Niebuhr and Maritain purport to maintain the autonomous status of history, but insist that the end or goal of history lies outside history. Personally, I find it hard to reconcile the integrity of history with belief in some super-historical force on which its meaning and significance depend — whether that force be the God of a Chosen People, a Christian God, the Hidden Hand of the Deist, or Hegel's World Spirit. For the purposes of these lectures, I shall assume that the historian must solve his problems without recourse to any such *deus ex machina*, that history is a game played, so to speak, without a joker in the pack.

The relation of history to morality is more complicated and discussions of it in the past have suffered from several ambiguities. It is scarcely necessary today to argue that the historian is not required to pass moral judgments on the private life of the characters in his story. The standpoints of the historian and of the moralist are not identical. Henry VIII may have been a bad husband and a good king. But the historian is interested in him in the former capacity only insofar as it affected historical events. If his moral delinquencies had had as little apparent effect on public affairs as those of Henry II, the historian would not need to bother about them. This goes for virtues as well as vices. Pasteur and Einstein were, one is told, men of exemplary, even saintly, private lives. But, suppose they had been unfaithful husbands, cruel fathers and unscrupulous colleagues, would their historical achievements have been any the less? And it is these which preoccupy the historian. Stalin is said to have behaved cruelly and callously to his second wife; but, as a historian of Soviet affairs, I do not feel myself much concerned. This does not mean that private morality is not important, or that the history of morals is not a legitimate part of history. But the historian does not turn aside to pronounce moral judgments on the private lives of individuals who appear in his pages. He has other things to do.

The more serious ambiguity arises over the question of moral judgments on public actions. Belief in the duty of the historian to pronounce moral judgments on his *dramatis personae* has a long pedigree. But it was never more powerful than in nineteenth-century Britain, when it was reinforced both by the moralizing tendencies of the age and by the uninhibited cult of individualism. Rosebery remarked that what English people wanted to know about Napoleon was whether he was 'a good man'.[1] Acton in his correspondence with Creighton declared that 'the inflexibility of the moral code is the secret of the authority, the dignity and the utility of History,' and claimed to make history 'an arbiter of controversy, a guide of the wanderer, the upholder of that moral standard which the powers of earth and of religion itself tend constantly to depress'[2] — a view based on Acton's almost mystical belief in the objectivity and supremacy of historical facts, which apparently requires and entitles the historian, in the name of History as a sort of super-historical power, to pass moral judgments on individuals participating in historical events. This attitude still sometimes reappears in unexpected forms. Professor Toynbee described Mussolini's invasion of Abyssinia in 1935 as a 'deliberate personal sin';[3] and Sir

[1] Rosebery, *Napoleon : The Last Phase*, p. 364.
[2] Acton, *Historical Essays and Studies* (1907), p. 505.
[3] *Survey of International Affairs*, 1935, ii, 3.

Isaiah Berlin in the essay already quoted insists with great vehemence that it is the duty of the historian 'to judge Charlemagne or Napoleon or Genghis Khan or Hitler or Stalin for their massacres'.[1] This view has been sufficiently castigated by Professor Knowles, who in his inaugural lecture quoted Motley's denunciation of Philip II ('if there are vices . . . from which he was exempt, it is because it is not permitted by human nature to attain perfection even in evil'), and Stubbs's description of King John ('polluted with every crime that could disgrace a man'), as instances of moral judgments on individuals which it is not within the competence of the historian to pronounce: 'The historian is not a judge, still less a hanging judge'.[2] But Croce also has a fine passage on this point which I should like to quote:

> The accusation forgets the great difference that our tribunals (whether juridical or moral) are present-day tribunals designed for living, active and dangerous men, while those other men have already appeared before the tribunal of their day, and cannot be condemned or absolved twice. They cannot be held responsible before any tribunal whatsoever, just because they are men of the past who belong to the peace of the past and as such can only be subjects of history, and can suffer no other judgment than that which penetrates and understands the spirit of their work. . . . Those who on the plea of narrating

[1] I. Berlin, *Historical Inevitability*, pp. 76-77. Sir Isaiah's attitude recalls the views of that sturdy nineteenth-century conservative jurist Fitzjames Stephen: 'The criminal law thus proceeds upon the principle that it is morally right to hate criminals. . . . It is highly desirable that criminals should be hated, that the punishments inflicted on them should be so contrived as to give expression to that hatred, and to justify it so far as the public provision of means for expressing and gratifying a healthy natural sentiment can justify and encourage it' (*A History of the Criminal Law of England* (1883), ii, 81-82, quoted in L. Radzinowicz, *Sir James Fitzjames Stephen* (1957), p. 30). These views are no longer widely shared by criminologists; but my quarrel with them here is that, whatever their validity elsewhere, they are not applicable to the verdicts of history.

[2] D. Knowles, *The Historian and Character* (1955), pp. 4-5, 12, 19.

history bustle about as judges, condemning here and giving absolution there, because they think that this is the office of history . . . are generally recognized as devoid of historical sense.[1]

And if anyone cavils at the statement that it is not our business to pass moral judgment on Hitler or Stalin — or, if you like, on Senator McCarthy — this is because they were the contemporaries of many of us, because hundreds of thousands of those who suffered directly or indirectly from their actions are still alive, and because, precisely for these reasons, it is difficult for us to approach them as historians and to divest ourselves of other capacities which might justify us in passing judgment on their deeds : this is one of the embarrassments — I should say, the principal embarrassment — of the contemporary historian. But what profit does anyone find today in denouncing the sins of Charlemagne or of Napoleon ?

Let us therefore reject the notion of the historian as a hanging judge, and turn to the more difficult but more profitable question of the passing of moral judgments not on individuals, but on events, institutions or policies of the past. These are the important judgments of the historian ; and those who insist so fervently on the moral condemnation of the individual sometimes unconsciously provide an alibi for whole groups and societies. The French historian Lefèbvre, seeking to exonerate the French revolution from responsibility for the disasters and bloodshed of the Napoleonic wars, attributed them to 'the dictatorship of a general . . . whose temperament . . . could not easily acquiesce in peace and moderation'.[2] Germans today welcome the denunciation of Hitler's individual wickedness as a satisfactory alternative to the moral judgment of the historian on the society which produced him. Russians, Englishmen and Americans readily join in personal attacks on Stalin, Neville Chamberlain or McCarthy as scapegoats for their collective misdeeds. Moreover laudatory

---

[1] B. Croce, *History as the Story of Liberty* (Engl. transl., 1941), p. 47.
[2] *Peuples et civilisations*, vol. xiv : *Napoléon*, p. 58.

moral judgments on individuals can be just as misleading and mischievous as the moral denunciation of individuals. Recognition that some individual slave-owners were high-minded was constantly used as an excuse for not condemning slavery as immoral. Max Weber refers to 'the masterless slavery in which capitalism enmeshes the worker or the debtor', and rightly argues that the historian should pass moral judgment on the institution, but not on the individuals who created it.[1] The historian does not sit in judgment on an individual oriental despot. But he is not required to remain indifferent and impartial between, say, oriental despotism and the institutions of Periclean Athens. He will not pass judgment on the individual slave-owner. But this does not prevent him from condemning a slave-owning society. Historical facts, as we saw, presuppose some measure of interpretation; and historical interpretations always involve moral judgments —or, if you prefer a more neutral-sounding term, value judgments.

This is, however, only the beginning of our difficulties. History is a process of struggle in which results, whether we judge them good or bad, are achieved by some groups directly or indirectly — and more often directly than indirectly — at the expense of others. The losers pay. Suffering is indigenous in history. Every great period of history has its casualties as well as its victories. This is an exceedingly complicated question because we have no measure which enables us to balance the greater good of some against the sacrifices of others: yet some such balance must be struck. It is not exclusively a problem of history. In ordinary life we are more often involved than we sometimes care to admit in the necessity of preferring the lesser evil, or of doing evil that good may come. In history the question is sometimes discussed under the rubric 'the cost of progress' or 'the price of revolution'. This is misleading. As Bacon says in the essay *On Innovations*, 'the froward retention of custom is as turbulent a thing as an innovation'. The cost of conservation

[1] Quoted in *From Max Weber : Essays in Sociology* (1947), p. 58.

falls just as heavily on the under-privileged as the cost of innovation on those who are deprived of their privileges. The
thesis that the good of some justifies the sufferings of others
is implicit in all government, and is just as much a conservative as a radical doctrine. Dr. Johnson robustly invoked
the argument of the lesser evil to justify the maintenance of
existing inequalities.

> It is better that some should be unhappy than that
> none should be happy, which would be the case in a
> general state of equality.[1]

But it is in periods of radical change that the issue appears in
its most dramatic form; and it is here that we find it easiest
to study the attitude of the historian towards it.

Let us take the story of the industrialization of Great
Britain between, say, about 1780 and 1870. Virtually every
historian will treat the industrial revolution, probably without
discussion, as a great and progressive achievement. He will
also describe the driving of the peasantry off the land, the
herding of workers in unhealthy factories and unsanitary
dwellings, the exploitation of child labour. He will probably
say that abuses occurred in the working of the system, and
that some employers were more ruthless than others, and will
dwell with some unction on the gradual growth of a humani-
tarian conscience once the system has become established.
But he will assume, again probably without saying it, that
measures of coercion and exploitation, at any rate in the first
stages, were an unavoidable part of the cost of industrialization. Nor have I ever heard of a historian who said that, in
view of the cost, it would have been better to stay the hand
of progress and not industrialize; if any such exists, he

---

[1] Boswell, *Life of Doctor Johnson*, A.D. 1776 (Everyman ed. ii, 20).
This has the merit of candour; Burckhardt (*Judgements on History and
Historians*, p. 85) sheds tears over the 'silenced moans' of the victims
of progress, 'who, as a rule, had wanted nothing else but *parta tueri*',
but is himself silent about the moans of the victims of the *ancien régime*
who, as a rule, had nothing to preserve.

doubtless belongs to the school of Chesterton and Belloc, and will — quite properly — not be taken seriously by serious historians. This example is of particular interest to me, because I hope soon in my history of Soviet Russia to approach the problem of the collectivization of the peasant as a part of the cost of industrialization ; and I know well that if, following the example of historians of the British industrial revolution, I deplore the brutalities and abuses of collectivization, but treat the process as an unavoidable part of the cost of a desirable and necessary policy of industrialization, I shall incur charges of cynicism and of condoning evil things. Historians condone the nineteenth-century colonization of Asia and Africa by the western nations on the ground not only of its immediate effects on the world economy, but of its long-term consequences for the backward peoples of these continents. After all, it is said, modern India is the child of British rule ; and modern China is the product of nineteenth-century western imperialism, crossed with the influence of the Russian revolution. Unfortunately it was not the Chinese workers who laboured in the western-owned factories in the treaty ports, or in the South African mines, or on the western front in the first World War, who have survived to enjoy whatever glory or profit may have accrued from the Chinese revolution. Those who pay the cost are rarely those who reap the benefits. The well-known purple passage from Engels is uncomfortably apt :

> History is about the most cruel of all goddesses, and she leads her triumphal car over heaps of corpses, not only in war, but also in 'peaceful' economic development. And we men and women are unfortunately so stupid that we never pluck up courage for real progress unless urged to it by sufferings that seem almost out of proportion.[1]

Ivan Karamazov's famous gesture of defiance is a heroic fallacy. We are born into society, we are born into history.

[1] Letter of February 24, 1893, to Danielson in *Karl Marx and Friedrich Engels : Correspondence 1846–1895* (1934), p. 510.

No moment occurs when we are offered a ticket of admission with the option to accept or reject it. The historian has no more conclusive answer than the theologian to the problem of suffering. He, too, falls back on the thesis of the lesser evil and the greater good.

But does not the fact that the historian, unlike the scientist, becomes involved by the nature of his material in these issues of moral judgment imply the submission of history to a super-historical standard of value? I do not think that it does. Let us assume that abstract conceptions like 'good' and 'bad', and more sophisticated developments of them, lie beyond the confines of history. But, even so, these abstractions play in the study of historical morality much the same role as mathematical and logical formulas in physical science. They are indispensable categories of thought; but they are devoid of meaning or application till specific content is put into them. If you prefer a different metaphor, the moral precepts which we apply in history or in everyday life are like cheques on a bank: they have a printed and a written part. The printed part consists of abstract words like liberty and equality, justice and democracy. These are essential categories. But the cheque is valueless until we fill in the other part, which states how much liberty we propose to allocate to whom, whom we recognize as our equals and up to what amount. The way in which we fill in the cheque from time to time is a matter of history. The process by which specific historical content is given to abstract moral conceptions is a historical process; indeed, our moral judgments are made within a conceptual framework which is itself the creation of history. The favourite form of contemporary international controversy on moral issues is a debate on rival claims to freedom and democracy. The conceptions are abstract and universal. But the content put into them has varied throughout history, from time to time and from place to place; any practical issue of their application can be understood and debated only in historical terms. To take a slightly less popular example, the attempt has been made to use the conception of 'economic rationality' as an objective and non-controversial criterion by which the desirability of economic policies can be tested and judged. The attempt at once breaks down. Theorists brought up on the laws of classical economics condemn planning in principle as an irrational intrusion into rational economic processes; for example, planners refuse in their price policy to be bound by the law of supply and demand, and prices under planning can have no rational basis. It may, of course, be true that planners often behave irrationally, and therefore foolishly. But the criterion by which they must be judged is not the old 'economic rationality' of classical economy. Personally, I have more sympathy with the converse argument that it was the uncontrolled, unorganized *laissez-faire* economy which was essentially irrational, and that planning is an attempt to introduce 'economic rationality' into the process. But the only point which I wish to make at the moment is the impossibility of erecting an abstract and super-historical standard by which historical actions can be judged. Both sides inevitably read into such a standard the specific content appropriate to their own historical conditions and aspirations.

This is the real indictment of those who seek to erect a super-historical standard or criterion in the light of which judgment is passed on historical events or situations — whether that standard derives from some divine authority postulated by the theologians, and from a static Reason or Nature postulated by the philosophers of the Enlightenment. It is not that shortcomings occur in the application of the standard, or defects in the standard itself. It is that the attempt to erect such a standard is unhistorical and contradicts the very essence of history. It provides a dogmatic answer to questions which the historian is bound by his vocation incessantly to ask : the historian who accepts answers in advance to these questions goes to work with his eyes blindfolded, and renounces his vocation. History is movement;

and movement implies comparison. That is why historians tend to express their moral judgments in words of a comparative nature like 'progressive' and 'reactionary' rather than in uncompromising absolutes like 'good' and 'bad'; these are attempts to define different societies or historical phenomena not in relation to some absolute standard, but in their relation to one another. Moreover, when we examine these supposedly absolute and extra-historical values, we find that they too are in fact rooted to history. The emergence of a particular value or ideal at a given time or place is explained by historical conditions of place and time. The practical content of hypothetical absolutes like equality, liberty, justice, or natural law varies from period to period, or from continent to continent. Every group has its own values which are rooted in history. Every group protects itself against the intrusion of alien and inconvenient values, which it brands by opprobrious epithets as bourgeois and capitalist, or undemocratic and totalitarian, or, more crudely still, as un-English and un-American. The abstract standard or value, divorced from society and divorced from history, is as much an illusion as the abstract individual. The serious historian is the one who recognizes the historically conditioned character of all values, not the one who claims for his own values an objectivity beyond history. The beliefs which we hold and the standards of judgment which we set up are part of history, and are as much subject to historical investigation as any other aspect of human behaviour. Few sciences today — least of all the social sciences — would lay claim to total independence. But history has no fundamental dependence on something outside itself which would differentiate it from any other science.

Let me sum up what I have tried to say about the claim of history to be included among the sciences. The word science already covers so many different branches of knowledge, employing so many different methods and techniques, that the onus seems to rest on those who seek to exclude history rather than on those who seek to include it. It is significant that the arguments for exclusion come not from scientists anxious to exclude historians from their select company, but from historians and philosophers anxious to vindicate the status of history as a branch of humane letters. The dispute reflects the prejudice of the old division between the humanities and science, in which the humanities were supposed to represent the broad culture of the ruling class, and science the skills of the technicians who served it. The words 'humanities' and 'humane' are themselves in this context a survival of this time-honoured prejudice; and the fact that the antithesis between science and history will not make sense in any language but English suggests the peculiarly insular character of the prejudice. My principal objection to the refusal to call history a science is that it justifies and perpetuates the rift between the so-called 'two cultures'. The rift itself is a product of this ancient prejudice, based on a class structure of English society which itself belongs to the past; and I am myself not convinced that the chasm which separates the historian from the geologist is any deeper or more unbridgeable than the chasm which separates the geologist from the physicist. But the way to mend the rift is not, in my view, to teach elementary science to historians or elementary history to scientists. This is a blind alley into which we have been led by muddled thinking. After all, scientists themselves do not behave in this way. I have never heard of engineers being advised to attend elementary classes in botany.

One remedy I would suggest is to improve the standard of our history, to make it — if I may dare to say so — more scientific, to make our demands on those who pursue it more rigorous. History as an academic discipline in this university is sometimes thought of as a catch-all for those who find classics too difficult and science too serious. One impression which I hope to convey in these lectures is that history is a far more difficult subject than classics, and quite as serious as any science. But this remedy would imply a stronger faith among historians themselves in what they are doing. Sir Charles Snow, in a recent lecture on this theme, had a point when he contrasted the 'brash' optimism of the scientist with the 'subdued voice' and 'anti-social feeling' of what he called the 'literary intellectual'.[1] Some historians — and more of those who write about history without being historians — belong to this category of 'literary intellectuals'. They are so busy telling us that history is not a science, and explaining what it cannot and should not be or do, that they have no time for its achievements and its potentialities.

The other way to heal the rift is to promote a profounder understanding of the identity of aim between scientists and historians; and this is the main value of the new and growing interest in the history and philosophy of science. Scientists, social scientists and historians are all engaged in different branches of the same study: the study of man and his environment, of the effects of man on his environment and of his environment on man. The object of the study is the same: to increase man's understanding of, and mastery over, his environment. The presuppositions and the methods of the physicist, the geologist, the psychologist and the historian differ widely in detail; nor do I wish to commit myself to the proposition that, in order to be more scientific, the historian must follow more closely the methods of physical science. But historian and physical scientist are united in the fundamental purpose of seeking to explain, and in the fundamental procedure of question and answer. The historian, like any other scientist, is an animal who incessantly asks the question, Why? In my next lecture I shall examine the ways in which he puts the question and in which he attempts to answer it.

[1] C. P. Snow, *The Two Cultures and the Scientific Revolution* (1959), pp. 4-8.

# IV

## Causation in History

IF milk is set to boil in a saucepan, it boils over. I do not know, and have never wanted to know, why this happens; if pressed, I should probably attribute it to a propensity in milk to boil over, which is true enough but explains nothing. But then I am not a natural scientist. In the same way, one can read, or even write, about the events of the past without wanting to know why they happened, or be content to say that the second World War occurred because Hitler wanted war, which is true enough but explains nothing. But one should not then commit the solecism of calling oneself a student of history or a historian. The study of history is a study of causes. The historian, as I said at the end of my last lecture, continuously asks the question, Why?; and, so long as he hopes for an answer, he cannot rest. The great historian — or perhaps I should say more broadly, the great thinker — is the man who asks the question, Why?, about new things or in new contexts.

Herodotus, the father of history, defined his purpose in the opening of his work : to preserve a memory of the deeds of the Greeks and the barbarians, 'and in particular, beyond everything else, to give the cause of their fighting one another'. He found few disciples in the ancient world : even Thucydides has been accused of having no clear conception of causation.[1] But when in the eighteenth century the foundations of modern historiography began to be laid, Montesquieu, in his *Considerations on the Causes of the Greatness of the Romans*

---

[1] F. M. Cornford, *Thucydides Mythistoricus*, *passim*.

*and of their Rise and Decline,* took as his starting-point the
principles that 'there are general causes, moral or physical,
which operate in every monarchy, raise it, maintain it, or
overthrow it', and that 'all that occurs is subject to these
causes'. A few years later in the *Esprit des lois* he developed
and generalized this idea. It was absurd to suppose that 'blind
fate has produced all the effects which we see in the world'.
Men were 'not governed uniquely by their fantasies'; their
behaviour followed certain laws or principles derived from
'the nature of things'.[1] For nearly 200 years after that, historians and philosophers of history were busily engaged in
an attempt to organize the past experience of mankind by
discovering the causes of historical events and the laws which
governed them. Sometimes the causes and the laws were
thought of in mechanical, sometimes in biological, terms,
sometimes as metaphysical, sometimes as economic, sometimes as psychological. But it was accepted doctrine that
history consisted in marshalling the events of the past in an
orderly sequence of cause and effect. 'If you have nothing
to tell us', wrote Voltaire in his article on history for the
Encyclopedia, 'except that one barbarian succeeded another
on the banks of the Oxus and Jaxartes, what is that to us?'
In the last years the picture has been somewhat modified.
Nowadays, for reasons discussed in my last lecture, we no
longer speak of historical 'laws'; and even the word 'cause'
has gone out of fashion, partly owing to certain philosophical
ambiguities into which I need not enter, and partly owing to
its supposed association with determinism, to which I will
come presently. Some people therefore speak not of 'cause'
in history, but of 'explanation' or 'interpretation', or of 'the
logic of the situation', or of 'the inner logic of events' (this
comes from Dicey), or reject the causal approach (why it
happened) in favour of the functional approach (how it happened), though this seems inevitably to involve the question
how it came to happen, and so leads us back to the question,

1 *De l'esprit des lois,* Preface and ch. 1.

Why? Other people distinguish between different kinds of cause — mechanical, biological, psychological and so forth — and regard historical cause as a category of its own. Though some of these distinctions are in some degree valid, it may be more profitable for present purposes to stress what is common to all kinds of cause, than what separates them. For myself, I shall be content to use the word 'cause' in the popular sense and neglect these particular refinements.

Let us begin by asking what the historian in practice does when he is confronted by the necessity of assigning causes to events. The first characteristic of the historian's approach to the problem of cause is that he will commonly assign several causes to the same event. Marshall the economist once wrote that 'people must be warned off by every possible means from considering the action of any one cause . . . without taking account of the others whose effects are commingled with it'.[1] The examination candidate who, in answering the question, 'Why did revolution break out in Russia in 1917 ?', offered only one cause, would be lucky to get a third class. The historian deals in a multiplicity of causes. If he were required to consider the causes of the Bolshevik revolution, he might name Russia's successive military defeats, the collapse of the Russian economy under pressure of war, the effective propaganda of the Bolsheviks, the failure of the Tsarist government to solve the agrarian problem, the concentration of an impoverished and exploited proletariat in the factories of Petrograd, the fact that Lenin knew his own mind and nobody on the other side did — in short, a random jumble of economic, political, ideological and personal causes, of long-term and short-term causes.

But this brings us at once to the second characteristic of the historian's approach. The candidate who, in reply to our question, was content to set out one after the other a dozen causes of the Russian revolution and leave it at that, might get a second class, but scarcely a first; 'well-informed, but

[1] *Memorials of Alfred Marshall*, ed. A. C. Pigou (1925), p. 428.

unimaginative' would probably be the verdict of the examiners. The true historian, confronted with this list of causes of his own compiling, would feel a professional compulsion to reduce it to order, to establish some hierarchy of causes which would fix their relation to one another, perhaps to decide which cause, or which category of causes, should be regarded 'in the last resort' or 'in the final analysis' (favourite phrases of historians) as the ultimate cause, the cause of all causes. This is his interpretation of his theme ; the historian is known by the causes which he invokes. Gibbon attributed the decline and fall of the Roman empire to the triumph of barbarism and religion. The English Whig historians of the nineteenth century attributed the rise of British power and prosperity to the development of political institutions embodying the principles of constitutional liberty. Gibbon and the English nineteenth-century historians have an old-fashioned look today because they ignore the economic causes which modern historians have moved into the forefront. Every historical argument revolves round the question of the priority of causes.

Henri Poincaré, in the work which I quoted in my last lecture, noted that science was advancing simultaneously 'towards variety and complexity' and 'towards unity and simplicity', and that this dual and apparently contradictory process was a necessary condition of knowledge.[1] This is no less true of history. The historian, by expanding and deepening his research, constantly accumulates more and more answers to the question, Why ? The proliferation in recent years of economic, social, cultural and legal history — not to mention fresh insights into the complexities of political history, and the new techniques of psychology and statistics — have enormously increased the number and range of our answers. When Bertrand Russell observed that 'every advance in a science takes us further away from the crude uniformities which are first observed into a greater differentiation of ante-

[1] H. Poincaré, *La Science et l'hypothèse* (1902), pp. 202-203.

cedent and consequent and into a continually wider circle of antecedents recognized as relevant',[1] he accurately described the situation in history. But the historian, in virtue of his urge to understand the past, is simultaneously compelled, like the scientist, to simplify the multiplicity of his answers, to subordinate one answer to another, and to introduce some order and unity into the chaos of happenings and the chaos of specific causes. 'One God, one Law, one Element, And one far-off divine event', or Henry Adams's quest for 'some great generalization which would finish one's clamour to be educated'[2] — these read nowadays like old-fashioned jokes. But the fact remains that the historian must work through the simplification, as well as through the multiplication, of causes. History, like science, advances through this dual and apparently contradictory process.

At this point I must reluctantly turn aside to deal with two savoury red herrings which have been drawn across our path — one labelled 'Determinism in History; or the Wickedness of Hegel', the other 'Chance in History; or Cleopatra's Nose'. First I must say a word or two about how they come to be here. Professor Karl Popper, who in the 1930s in Vienna wrote a weighty work on the new look in science, recently translated into English under the title *The Logic of Scientific Enquiry*, published in English during the war two books of a more popular character: *The Open Society and Its Enemies* and *The Poverty of Historicism*.[3] They were written under the strong emotional influence of the reaction against Hegel, who was treated, together with Plato, as the spiritual ancestor of Nazism, and against the rather shallow Marxism which was the intellectual climate of the British Left in the 1930s. The principal targets were the allegedly determinist philosophies of history of Hegel and Marx grouped together

---

[1] B. Russell, *Mysticism and Logic* (1918), p. 188.
[2] *The Education of Henry Adams* (Boston, 1928), p. 224.
[3] *The Poverty of Historicism* was first published in book form in 1957, but consists of articles originally published in 1944 and 1945.

under the opprobrious name of 'Historicism'.[1] In 1954 Sir Isaiah Berlin published his essay on *Historical Inevitability*. He dropped the attack on Plato, perhaps out of some lingering respect for that ancient pillar of the Oxford Establishment;[2] and he added to the indictment the argument, not found in Popper, that the 'historicism' of Hegel and Marx is objectionable because, by explaining human actions in causal terms, it implies a denial of human free will, and encourages historians to evade their supposed obligation, of which I spoke in my last lecture, to pronounce moral condemnation on the Charlemagnes, Napoleons and Stalins of history. Otherwise not much has changed. But Sir Isaiah Berlin is a deservedly popular and widely read writer. During the past five or six years, almost everyone in this country or in the United States who has written an article about history, or even a serious review of a historical work, has cocked a knowing snook at Hegel and Marx and determinism, and pointed out the absurdity

[1] I have avoided the word 'historicism' except in one or two places where precision was not required, since Professor Popper's widely read writings on the subject have emptied the term of precise meaning. Constant insistence on the definition of terms is pedantic. But one must know what one is talking about, and Professor Popper uses 'historicism' as a catch-all for any opinion about history which he dislikes, including some which seem to me sound and others which are, I suspect, held by no serious writer today. As he admits (*The Poverty of Historicism*, p. 3), he invents 'historicist' arguments which have never been used by any known 'historicist'. In his writing, historicism covers both doctrines which assimilate history to science, and doctrines which sharply differentiate the two. In *The Open Society*, Hegel, who avoided prediction, is treated as the high-priest of historicism ; in the introduction to *The Poverty of Historicism*, historicism is described as 'an approach to the social sciences which assumes that *historical prediction* is their principal aim'. Hitherto 'historicism' has been commonly used as the English version of the German 'Historismus' ; now Professor Popper distinguishes 'historicism' from 'historism', thus adding a further element of confusion to the already confused usage of the term. M. C. D'Arcy, *The Sense of History: Secular and Sacred* (1959), p. 11, uses the word historicism' as 'identical with a philosophy of history'.

[2] The attack on Plato as the first Fascist originated, however, in a series of broadcasts by an Oxford man, R. H. Crossman, *Plato Today* (1937).

of failing to recognize the role of accident in history. It is perhaps unfair to hold Sir Isaiah responsible for his disciples. Even when he talks nonsense, he earns our indulgence by talking it in an engaging and attractive way. The disciples repeat the nonsense, and fail to make it attractive. In any case, there is nothing new in all this. Charles Kingsley, not the most distinguished of our Regius Professors of Modern History, who had probably never read Hegel or heard of Marx, spoke in his inaugural lecture in 1860 of man's 'mysterious power of breaking the laws of his own being' as proof that no 'inevitable sequence' could exist in history.[1] But fortunately we had forgotten Kingsley. It is Professor Popper and Sir Isaiah Berlin who between them have flogged this very dead horse back into a semblance of life; and some patience will be required to clear up the muddle.

First then let me take determinism, which I will define — I hope, uncontroversially — as the belief that everything that happens has a cause or causes, and could not have happened differently unless something in the cause or causes had also been different.[2] Determinism is a problem not of history, but of all human behaviour. The human being whose actions have no cause and are therefore undetermined is as much an abstraction as the individual outside society whom we discussed in a previous lecture. Professor Popper's assertion that 'everything is possible in human affairs'[3] is either meaningless or false. Nobody in ordinary life believes or can believe this. The axiom that everything has a cause is a condition of our capacity to understand what is going on

[1] C. Kingsley, *The Limits of Exact Science as Applied to History* (1860), p. 22.
[2] 'Determinism . . . means . . . that, the data being what they are, whatever happens happens definitely and could not be different. To hold that it could, means only that it would if the data were different' (S. W Alexander in *Essays Presented to Ernst Cassirer* (1936), p. 18).
[3] K. R. Popper, *The Open Society* (2nd ed., 1952), ii, 197.

around us.[1]   The nightmare quality of Kafka's novels lies in the fact that nothing that happens has any apparent cause, or any cause that can be ascertained : this leads to the total disintegration of the human personality, which is based on the assumption that events have causes, and that enough of these causes are ascertainable to build up in the human mind a pattern of past and present sufficiently coherent to serve as a guide to action.   Everyday life would be impossible unless one assumed that human behaviour was determined by causes which are in principle ascertainable.   Once upon a time some people thought it blasphemous to enquire into the causes of natural phenomena, since these were obviously governed by the divine will.   Sir Isaiah Berlin's objection to our explaining why human beings acted as they did, on the ground that these actions are governed by the human will, belongs to the same order of ideas, and perhaps indicates that the social sciences are in the same stage of development today as were the natural sciences when this kind of argument was directed against them.

Let us see how we handle this problem in everyday life. As you go about your daily affairs, you are in the habit of meeting Smith. You greet him with an amiable, but pointless, remark about the weather, or about the state of college or university business ; he replies with an equally amiable and pointless remark about the weather or the state of business. But supposing that one morning Smith, instead of answering your remark in his usual way, were to break into a violent diatribe against your personal appearance or character. Would you shrug your shoulders, and treat this as a convincing demonstration of the freedom of Smith's will and of the fact that everything is possible in human affairs ?   I suspect that

[1] 'The Law of Causality is not imposed upon us by the world', but 'is perhaps for us the most convenient method of adapting ourselves to the world' (J. Rueff, *From the Physical to the Social Sciences* (Baltimore, 1929), p. 52) ; Professor Popper himself (*The Logic of Scientific Enquiry*, p. 248) calls belief in causality a 'metaphysical hypostatization of a well-justified methodological rule'.

you would not. On the contrary, you would probably say something like: 'Poor Smith ! You know, of course, his father died in a mental hospital', or 'Poor Smith! He must have been having more trouble with his wife'. In other words, you would attempt to diagnose the cause of Smith's apparently causeless behaviour in the firm conviction that some cause there must be. By so doing you would, I fear, incur the wrath of Sir Isaiah Berlin, who would bitterly complain that, by providing a causal explanation of Smith's behaviour, you had swallowed Hegel's and Marx's deterministic assumption, and shirked your obligation to denounce Smith as a cad. But nobody in ordinary life takes this view, or supposes that either determinism or moral responsibility is at stake. The logical dilemma about free will and determinism does not arise in real life. It is not that some human actions are free and others determined. The fact is that all human actions are both free and determined, according to the point of view from which one considers them. The practical question is different again. Smith's action had a cause, or a number of causes ; but in so far as it was caused not by some external compulsion, but by the compulsion of his own personality, he was morally responsible, since it is a condition of social life that normal adult human beings are morally responsible for their own personality. Whether to hold him responsible in this particular case is a matter for your practical judgment. But, if you do, this does not mean that you regard his action as having no cause : cause and moral responsibility are different categories. An Institute and Chair of Criminology have recently been established in this university. It would not, I feel sure, occur to any of those engaged in investigating the causes of crime to suppose that this committed them to a denial of the moral responsibility of the criminal.

Now let us look at the historian. Like the ordinary man, he believes that human actions have causes which are in principle ascertainable. History, like everyday life, would be impossible if this assumption were not made. It is the special function of the historian to investigate these causes. This may be thought to give him a special interest in the determined aspect of human behaviour: but he does not reject free will — except on the untenable hypothesis that voluntary actions have no cause. Nor is he troubled by the question of inevitability. Historians, like other people, sometimes fall into rhetorical language and speak of an occurrence as 'inevitable' when they mean merely that the conjunction of factors leading one to expect it was overwhelmingly strong. Recently I searched my own history for the offending word, and cannot give myself an entirely clean bill of health: in one passage I wrote that, after the revolution of 1917, a clash between the Bolsheviks and the Orthodox Church was 'inevitable'. No doubt it would have been wiser to say 'extremely probable'. But may I be excused for finding the correction a shade pedantic? In practice, historians do not assume that events are inevitable before they have taken place. They frequently discuss alternative courses available to the actors in the story on the assumption that the option was open, though they go on quite correctly to explain why one course was eventually chosen rather than the other. Nothing in history is inevitable except in the formal sense that, for it to have happened otherwise, the antecedent causes would have had to be different. As a historian, I am perfectly prepared to do without 'inevitable', 'unavoidable', 'inescapable' and even 'ineluctable'. Life will be drabber. But let us leave them to poets and metaphysicians.

So barren and pointless does this charge of inevitability appear, and so great the vehemence with which it has been pursued in recent years, that I think we must look for the hidden motives behind it. Its principal source is, I suspect, what I may call the 'might-have-been' school of thought — or rather of emotion. It attaches itself almost exclusively to contemporary history. Last term here in Cambridge I saw a talk to some society advertised under the title 'Was the Russian Revolution Inevitable?' I am sure it was intended as a perfectly serious talk. But if you had seen a talk advertised on 'Were the Wars of the Roses Inevitable ?' you would at once have suspected some joke. The historian writes of the Norman Conquest or the American War of Independence as if what happened was in fact bound to happen, and as if it was his business simply to explain what happened and why ; and nobody accuses him of being a determinist and of failing to discuss the alternative possibility that William the Conqueror or the American insurgents might have been defeated. When, however, I write about the Russian revolution of 1917 in precisely this way — the only proper way to the historian — I find myself under attack from my critics for having by implication depicted what happened as something that was bound to happen, and failed to examine all the other things that might have happened. Suppose, it is said, that Stolypin had had time to complete his agrarian reform, or that Russia had not gone to war, perhaps the revolution would not have occurred ; or suppose that the Kerensky government had made good, and that the leadership of the revolution had been assumed by the Mensheviks or the Social Revolutionaries instead of by the Bolsheviks. These suppositions are theoretically conceivable ; and one can always play a parlour game with the might-have-beens of history. But they have nothing to do with determinism ; for the determinist will only reply that, for these things to have happened, the causes would also have had to be different. Nor have they anything to do with history. The point is that today nobody seriously wishes to reverse the results of the Norman Conquest or of American independence or to express a passionate protest against these events ; and nobody objects when the historian treats them as a closed chapter. But plenty of people, who have suffered directly or vicariously from the results of the Bolshevik victory, or still fear its remoter consequences, desire to register their protest against it ; and this takes the form, when they read history, of letting their imagination run riot on all the more agreeable things that might have happened, and of being indignant with the historian who goes on quietly with his job of explaining what did happen and why their agreeable wish-dreams remain unfulfilled. The trouble about contemporary history is that people remember the time when all the options were still open, and find it difficult to adopt the attitude of the historian for whom they have been closed by the *fait accompli*. This is a purely emotional and unhistorical reaction. But it has furnished most of the fuel for the recent campaign against the supposed doctrine of 'historical inevitability'. Let us get rid of this red herring once and for all.

The other source of the attack is the famous crux of Cleopatra's nose. This is the theory that history is, by and large, a chapter of accidents, a series of events determined by chance coincidences, and attributable only to the most casual causes. The result of the Battle of Actium was due not to the sort of causes commonly postulated by historians, but to Antony's infatuation with Cleopatra. When Bajazet was deterred by an attack of gout from marching into central Europe, Gibbon observed that 'an acrimonious humour falling on a single fibre of one man may prevent or suspend the misery of nations'.[1] When King Alexander of Greece died in the autumn of 1920 from the bite of a pet monkey, this accident touched off a train of events which led Sir Winston Churchill to remark that 'a quarter of a million persons died of this monkey's bite'.[2] Or take again Trotsky's comment on the fever contracted while shooting ducks which put him out of action at a critical point of his quarrel with Zinoviev, Kamenev and Stalin in the autumn of 1923 : 'One can foresee a revolution or a war, but it is impossible to foresee the consequences of an autumn shooting-trip for wild ducks'.[3] The first thing to be made clear is that this question has nothing to do with the issue of determinism. Antony's infatuation with Cleopatra, or Bajazet's attack of gout, or Trotsky's

[1] *Decline and Fall of the Roman Empire*, ch. lxiv.
[2] W. Churchill, *The World Crisis : The Aftermath* (1929), p. 386.
[3] L. Trotsky, *My Life* (Engl. trans., 1930), p. 425.

feverish chill, were just as much causally determined as anything else that happens. It is unnecessarily discourteous to
Cleopatra's beauty to suggest that Antony's infatuation had
no cause. The connexion between female beauty and male
infatuation is one of the most regular sequences of cause and
effect observable in everyday life. These so-called accidents
in history represent a sequence of cause and effect interrupting
— and, so to speak, clashing with — the sequence which the
historian is primarily concerned to investigate. Bury, quite
rightly, speaks of a 'collision of two independent causal
chains'.[1] Sir Isaiah Berlin, who opens his essay on *Historical
Inevitability* by citing with praise an article of Bernard Berenson
on 'The Accidental View of History', is one of those who
confuse accident in this sense with an absence of causal deter-
mination. But, this confusion apart, we have a real problem
on our hands. How can one discover in history a coherent
sequence of cause and effect, how can we find any meaning in
history, when our sequence is liable to be broken or deflected
at any moment by some other, and from our point of view
irrelevant, sequence?

We may pause here for a moment to notice the origin
of this recent widespread insistence on the role of chance in
history. Polybius appears to have been the first historian to
occupy himself with it in any systematic way; and Gibbon
was quick to unmask the reason. 'The Greeks', observed
Gibbon, 'after their country had been reduced to a province,
imputed the triumphs of Rome not to the merit, but to the
fortune, of the republic.'[2] Tacitus, also a historian of the
decay of his country, was another ancient historian to indulge

[1] For Bury's argument on this point see *The Idea of Progress* (1920),
pp. 303-304.
[2] *Decline and Fall of the Roman Empire*, ch. 38. It is amusing to
note that the Greeks, after their conquest by the Romans, also indulged
in the game of historical 'might-have-beens' — the favourite consolation
of the defeated: if Alexander the Great had not died young, they told
themselves, 'he would have conquered the West and Rome would have
become subject to Greek kings' (K. von Fritz, *The Theory of the Mixed
Constitution in Antiquity* (N.Y., 1954), p. 395).

in extensive reflexions on chance. The renewed insistence by British writers on the importance of accident in history dates from the growth of a mood of uncertainty and apprehension which set in with the present century and became marked after 1914. The first British historian to sound this note after a long interval appears to have been Bury, who, in an article of 1909 on 'Darwinism in History', drew attention to 'the element of chance coincidence' which in large measure 'helps to determine events in social evolution'; and a separate article was devoted to this theme in 1916 under the title 'Cleopatra's Nose'.[1] H. A. L. Fisher in the passage already quoted, which reflects his disillusionment over the failure of iberal dreams after the first World War, begs his readers to recognize 'the play of the contingent and the unforseen' in history.[2] The popularity in this country of a theory of history as a chapter of accidents has coincided with the rise in France of a school of philosophers who preach that existence — I quote Sartre's famous *L'Être et le néant* — has 'neither cause nor reason nor necessity'. In Germany, the veteran historian Meinecke, as we have already noted, became impressed towards the end of his life with the role of chance in history. He reproached Ranke with not having paid sufficient attention to it; and after the second World War he attributed the national disasters of the past forty years to a series of accidents, the vanity of the Kaiser, the election of Hindenburg to the presidency of the Weimar republic, Hitler's obsessional character, and so forth — the bankruptcy of a great historian's

---

[1] Both articles are reprinted in J. B. Bury, *Selected Essays* (1930); for Collingwood's comments on Bury's views, see *The Idea of History*, pp. 148-150.

[2] For the passage, see p. 37 above. Toynbee's quotation of Fisher's dictum in *A Study of History*, v, 414, reveals a complete misapprehension: he regards it as a product of the 'modern Western belief in the omnipotence of chance', which 'gave birth' to *laissez-faire*. The theorists of *laissez-faire* believed not in chance, but in the hidden hand which imposed beneficent regularities on the diversity of human behaviour; and Fisher's remark was a product not of *laissez-faire* liberalism, but of its breakdown in the 1920s and 1930s.

mind under the stress of the misfortunes of his country.[1]   In a group or a nation which is riding in the trough, not on the crest, of historical events, theories that stress the role of chance or accident in history will be found to prevail.   The view that examination results are all a lottery will always be popular among those who have been placed in the third class.

But to uncover the sources of a belief is not to dispose of it; and we have still to discover exactly what Cleopatra's nose is doing in the pages of history.   Montesquieu was apparently the first who attempted to defend the laws of history against this intrusion.   'If a particular cause, like the accidental result of a battle, has ruined a state', he wrote in his work on the greatness and decline of the Romans, 'there was a general cause which made the downfall of this state ensue from a single battle.'   The Marxists also had some difficulty over this question.   Marx wrote of it only once, and that only in a letter:

> World history would have a very mystical character if there were no room in it for chance.   This chance itself naturally becomes part of the general trend of development and is compensated by other forms of chance.   But acceleration and retardation depend on such 'accidentals', which include the 'chance' character of the individuals who are at the head of a movement at the outset.[2]

Marx thus offered an apology for chance in history under three heads.   First, it was not very important; it could 'accelerate' or 'retard', but not, by implication, radically alter, the course of events.   Second, one chance was compensated by another, so that in the end chance cancelled itself out. Third, chance was especially illustrated in the character of individuals.[3]   Trotsky reinforced the theory of compensating

[1] The relevant passages are quoted by W. Stark in his introduction to F. Meinecke, *Machiavellism*, pp. xxxv–xxxvi.
[2] Marx and Engels, *Works* (Russian ed.), xxvi, 108.
[3] Tolstoy in *War and Peace*, Epilogue i, equated 'chance' and 'genius' as terms expressive of human inability to understand ultimate causes.

and self-cancelling accidents by an ingenious analogy :

> The entire historical process is a refraction of historical law through the accidental. In the language of biology, we might say that the historical law is realized through the natural selection of accidents.[1]

I confess that I find this theory unsatisfying and unconvincing. The role of accident in history is nowadays seriously exaggerated by those who are interested to stress its importance. But it exists, and to say that it merely accelerates or retards, but does not alter, is to juggle with words. Nor do I see any reason to believe that an accidental occurrence — say, the premature death of Lenin at the age of 54 — is automatically compensated by some other accident in such a way as to restore the balance of the historical process.

Equally inadequate is the view that accident in history is merely the measure of our ignorance — simply a name for something which we fail to understand.[2] This no doubt sometimes happens. The planets got their name, which means of course 'wanderers', when they were supposed to wander at random through the sky, and the regularity of their movements was not understood. To describe something as a mischance is a favourite way of exempting oneself from the tiresome obligation to investigate its cause ; and, when somebody tells me that history is a chapter of accidents, I tend to suspect him of intellectual laziness or low intellectual vitality. It is common practice with serious historians to point out that something hitherto treated as accidental was not an accident at all, but can be rationally explained and significantly fitted into the broader pattern of events. But this also does not fully answer our question. Accident is not simply something which we fail to understand. The solution of the prob-

[1] L. Trotsky, *My Life* (1930), p. 422.
[2] Tolstoy took this view : 'We are forced to fall back on fatalism as an explanation of irrational events, that is to say, of events the rationality of which we do not understand' (*War and Peace*, Bk. IX, ch. i) ; see also the passage cited on p. 95, note 3.

lem of accident in history must, I believe, be sought in a quite different order of ideas.

At an earlier stage we saw that history begins with the selection and marshalling of facts by the historian to become historical facts. Not all facts are historical facts. But the distinction between historical and unhistorical facts is not rigid or constant; and any fact may, so to speak, be promoted to the status of an historical fact once its relevance and significance is discerned. We now see that a somewhat similar process is at work in the historian's approach to causes. The relation of the historian to his causes has the same dual and reciprocal character as the relation of the historian to his facts. The causes determine his interpretation of the historical process, and his interpretation determines his selection and marshalling of the causes. The hierarchy of causes, the relative significance of one cause or set of causes or of another, is the essence of his interpretation. And this furnishes the clue to the problem of the accidental in history. The shape of Cleopatra's nose, Bajazet's attack of gout, the monkey-bite that killed King Alexander, the death of Lenin — these were accidents which modified the course of history. It is futile to attempt to spirit them away, or to pretend that in some way or other they had no effect. On the other hand, in so far as they were accidental, they do not enter into any rational interpretation of history, or into the historian's hierarchy of significant causes. Professor Popper and Professor Berlin — I cite them once more as the most distinguished and widely read representatives of the school — assume that the historian's attempt to find significance in the historical process and to draw conclusions from it is tantamount to an attempt to reduce 'the whole of experience' to a symmetrical order, and that the presence of accident in history dooms any such attempt to failure. But no sane historian pretends to do anything so fantastic as to embrace 'the whole of experience'; he cannot embrace more than a minute fraction of the facts even of his chosen sector or aspect of history. The world of the historian, like the world of the scientist, is not a photographic copy of the real world, but rather a working model which enables him more or less effectively to understand it and to master it. The historian distils from the experience of the past, or from so much of the experience of the past as is accessible to him, that part which he recognizes as amenable to rational explanation and interpretation, and from it draws conclusions which may serve as a guide to action. A recent popular writer, speaking of the achievements of science, refers graphically to the processes of the human mind which, 'rummaging in the ragbag of observed "facts", selects, pieces and patterns the *relevant* observed facts together, rejecting the *irrelevant*, until it has sewn together a logical and rational quilt of "knowledge".'[1] With some qualification as to the dangers of undue subjectivism, I should accept that as a picture of the way in which the mind of the historian works.

This procedure may puzzle and shock philosophers, and even some historians. But it is perfectly familiar to ordinary people going about the practical business of life. Let me illustrate. Jones, returning from a party at which he has consumed more than his usual ration of alcohol, in a car whose brakes turn out to have been defective, at a blind corner where visibility is notoriously poor, knocks down and kills Robinson, who was crossing the road to buy cigarettes at the shop on the corner. After the mess has been cleared up, we meet — say, at local police headquarters — to enquire into the causes of the occurrence. Was it due to the driver's semi-intoxicated condition — in which case there might be criminal prosecution? Or was it due to the defective brakes — in which case something might be said to the garage which overhauled the car only the week before? Or was it due to the blind corner — in which case the road authorities might be invited to give the matter their attention? While we are discussing these practical questions, two distinguished gentlemen — I shall not attempt to identify them — burst into the

[1] L. Paul, *The Annihilation of Man*, (1944), p. 147.

room and begin to tell us, with great fluency and cogency, that, if Robinson had not happened to run out of cigarettes that evening, he would not have been crossing the road and would not have been killed; that Robinson's desire for cigarettes was therefore the cause of his death; and that any enquiry which neglects this cause will be waste of time, and any conclusions drawn from it meaningless and futile. Well, what do we do? As soon as we can break into the flow of eloquence, we edge our two visitors gently but firmly towards the door, we instruct the janitor on no account to admit them again, and we get on with our enquiry. But what answer have we to the interrupters? Of course, Robinson was killed because he was a cigarette-smoker. Everything that the devotees of chance and contingency in history say is perfectly true and perfectly logical. It has the kind of remorseless logic which we find in *Alice in Wonderland* and *Through the Looking-Glass*. But, while I yield to none in my admiration for these ripe examples of Oxford scholarship, I prefer to keep my different modes of logic in separate compartments. The Dodgsonian mode is not the mode of history.

History therefore is a process of selection in terms of historical significance. To borrow Talcott Parsons's phrase once more, history is 'a selective system' not only of cognitive, but of causal, orientations to reality. Just as from the infinite ocean of facts the historian selects those which are significant for his purpose, so from the multiplicity of sequences of cause and effect he extracts those, and only those, which are historically significant; and the standard of historical significance is his ability to fit them into his pattern of rational explanation and interpretation. Other sequences of cause and effect have to be rejected as accidental, not because the relation between cause and effect is different, but because the sequence itself is irrelevant. The historian can do nothing with it; it is not amenable to rational interpretation, and has no meaning either for the past or the present. It is true that Cleopatra's nose, or Bajazet's gout, or Alexander's monkey-bite, or Lenin's death, or Robinson's cigarette-smoking, had results. But it makes no sense as a general proposition to say that generals lose battles because they are infatuated with beautiful queens, or that wars occur because kings keep pet monkeys, or that people get run over and killed on the roads because they smoke cigarettes. If on the other hand you tell the ordinary man that Robinson was killed because the driver was drunk, or because the brakes did not work, or because there was a blind corner on the road, this will seem to him a perfectly sensible and rational explanation; if he chooses to discriminate, he may even say that this, and not Robinson's desire for cigarettes, was the 'real' cause of Robinson's death. Similarly, if you tell the student of history that the struggles in the Soviet Union in the 1920s were due to discussions about the rate of industrialization, or about the best means of inducing the peasants to grow grain to feed the towns, or even to the personal ambitions of rival leaders, he will feel that these are rational and historically significant explanations in the sense that they could also be applied to other historical situations, and that they are 'real' causes of what happened in the sense that the accident of Lenin's premature death was not. He may even, if he is given to reflexion on these things, be reminded of Hegel's much quoted and much misunderstood dictum in the introduction to the *Philosophy of Right* that 'what is rational is real, and what is real is rational'.

Let us return for a moment to the causes of Robinson's death. We had no difficulty in recognizing that some of the causes were rational and 'real' and that others were irrational and accidental. But by what criterion did we make the distinction? The faculty of reason is normally exercised for some purpose. Intellectuals may sometimes reason, or think that they reason, for fun. But, broadly speaking, human beings reason to an end. And when we recognized certain explanations as rational, and other explanations as not rational, we were, I suggest, distinguishing between explanations which served some end and explanations which did not. In the case under discussion it made sense to suppose that the curbing of alcoholic indulgence in drivers, or a stricter control over the condition of brakes, or an improvement in the siting of roads, might serve the end of reducing the number of traffic fatalities. But it made no sense at all to suppose that the number of traffic fatalities could be reduced by preventing people from smoking cigarettes. This was the criterion by which we made our distinction. And the same goes for our attitude to causes in history. There, too, we distinguish between rational and accidental causes. The former, since they are potentially applicable to other countries, other periods and other conditions, lead to fruitful generalizations and lessons can be learned from them; they serve the end of broadening and deepening our understanding.[1] Accidental causes cannot be generalized; and, since they are in the fullest sense of the word unique, they teach no lessons and lead to no conclusions. But here I must make another point. It is precisely this notion of an end in view which provides the key to our treatment of causation in history; and this necessarily involves value judgments. Interpretation in history is, as we saw in the last lecture, always bound up with value judgments, and causality is bound up with interpretation. In the words of Meinecke — the great Meinecke, the Meinecke of the 1920s — 'the search for causalities in history is impossible without reference to values . . . behind the search for causalities there always lies, directly or indirectly, the search for values'.[2] And this recalls what I said earlier, about the dual and reciprocal function of history — to promote our understanding of the

---

[1] Professor Popper at one moment stumbles on this point but fails to see it. Having assumed 'a plurality of interpretations which are fundamentally on the same level of both suggestiveness and arbitrariness' (whatever exactly these two words imply), he adds in a parenthesis that 'some of them may be distinguished by their fertility — a point of some importance' (*The Poverty of Historicism*, p. 151), It is not *a* point of some importance: it is *the* point, which proves that 'historicism' (in some meanings of the term) is not so poor after all.

[2] *Kausalitäten und Werte in der Geschichte* (1928), translated in F. Stern, *Varieties of History* (1957), pp. 268, 273.

past in the light of the present and of the present in the light of the past. Anything which, like Antony's infatuation with Cleopatra's nose, fails to contribute to this dual purpose is from the point of view of the historian dead and barren.

At this juncture, it is time for me to confess to a rather shabby trick which I have played on you, though, since you will have had no difficulty in seeing through it, and since it has enabled me on several occasions to shorten and simplify what I had to say, you will perhaps have been indulgent enough to treat it as a convenient piece of shorthand. I have hitherto consistently used the conventional phrase 'past and present'. But, as we all know, the present has no more than a notional existence as an imaginary dividing line between the past and the future. In speaking of the present, I have already smuggled another time dimension into the argument. It would, I think, be easy to show that, since past and future are part of the same time-span, interest in the past and interest in the future are interconnected. The line of demarcation between pre-historic and historical times is crossed when people cease to live only in the present, and become consciously interested both in their past and in their future. History begins with the handing down of tradition ; and tradition means the carrying of the habits and lessons of the past into the future. Records of the past begin to be kept for the benefit of future generations. 'Historical thinking', writes the Dutch historian Huizinga, 'is always teleological.'[1] Sir Charles Snow recently wrote of Rutherford that 'like all scientists . . . he had, almost without thinking what it meant, the future in his bones'.[2] Good historians, I suspect, whether they think about it or not, have the future in their bones. Besides the question, Why ?, the historian also asks the question, Whither ?

[1] J. Huizinga translated in *Varieties of History*, ed. F. Stern (1957), p. 293.
[2] *The Baldwin Age*, ed. John Raymond (1960), p. 246.

# V

## History as Progress

LET me begin by quoting a passage from Professor Powicke's inaugural lecture as Regius Professor in Modern History in Oxford thirty years ago :

> The craving for an interpretation of history is so deep-rooted that, unless we have a constructive outlook over the past, we are drawn either to mysticism or to cynicism.[1]

'Mysticism' will, I think, stand for the view that the meaning of history lies somewhere outside history, in the realms of theology or eschatology — the view of such writers as Berdyaev or Niebuhr or Toynbee.[2] 'Cynicism' stands for the view, examples of which I have several times quoted, that history has no meaning, or a multiplicity of equally valid or invalid meanings, or the meaning which we arbitrarily choose to give to it. These are perhaps the two most popular views of history today. But I shall unhesitatingly reject both of them. This leaves us with that odd, but suggestive, phrase 'a constructive outlook over the past'. Having no way of knowing what was in Professor Powicke's mind when he used the phrase, I shall attempt to read my own interpretation into it.

Like the ancient civilizations of Asia, the classical civilization of Greece and Rome was basically unhistorical. As we have already seen, Herodotus as the father of history had few children ; and the writers of classical antiquity were on the

---

[1] F. Powicke, *Modern Historians and the Study of History* (1955), p. 174.
[2] 'History passes over into theology', as Toynbee triumphantly asserted (*Civilization on Trial* (1948), preface).

whole as little concerned with the future as with the past. Thucydides believed that nothing significant had happened in time before the events which he described, and that nothing significant was likely to happen thereafter. Lucretius deduced man's indifference to the future from his indifference to the past :

> Consider how that past ages of eternal time before our birth were no concern of ours. This is a mirror which nature holds up to us of future time after our death.[1]

Poetic visions of a brighter future took the form of visions of a return to a golden age of the past — a cyclical view which assimilated the processes of history to the processes of nature. History was not going anywhere : because there was no sense of the past, there was equally no sense of the future. Only Virgil, who in his fourth eclogue had given the classical picture of a return to the golden age, was inspired in the *Aeneid* momentarily to break through the cyclical conception : '*Imperium sine fine dedi*' was a most unclassical thought, which later earned Virgil recognition as a quasi-Christian prophet.

It was the Jews, and after them the Christians, who introduced an entirely new element by postulating a goal towards which the historical process is moving — the teleological view of history. History thus acquired a meaning and purpose, but at the expense of losing its secular character. The attainment of the goal of history would automatically mean the end of history : history itself became a theodicy. This was the mediaeval view of history. The Renaissance restored the classical view of an anthropocentric world and of the primacy of reason, but for the pessimistic classical view of the future substituted an optimistic view derived from the Jewish-Christian tradition. Time, which had once been hostile and corroding, now became friendly and creative : contrast Horace's '*Damnosa quid non imminuit dies ?*' with Bacon's '*Veritas temporis filia*'. The rationalists of the Enlighten-

---

[1] *De Rerum Natura*, iii, 992-995.

ment, who were the founders of modern historiography, re-
tained the Jewish-Christian teleological view, but secularized
the goal; they were thus enabled to restore the rational
character of the historical process itself. History became progress towards the goal of the perfection of man's estate on
earth. Gibbon, the greatest of the Enlightenment historians,
was not deterred by the nature of his subject from recording
what he called 'the pleasing conclusion that every age of
the world has increased, and still increases, the real wealth,
the happiness, the knowledge, and perhaps the virtue, of the
human race'.[1] The cult of progress reached its climax at the
moment when British prosperity, power and self-confidence
were at their height; and British writers and British historians
were among the most ardent votaries of the cult. The phenomenon is too familiar to need illustration; and I need only
quote one or two passages to show how recently faith in
progress remained a postulate of all our thinking. Acton, in
the report of 1896 on the project of the *Cambridge Modern
History* which I quoted in my first lecture, referred to history
as 'a progressive science'; and in the introduction to the
first volume of the history wrote that 'we are bound to assume,
as the scientific hypothesis on which history is to be written,
a progress in human affairs'. In the last volume of the history,
published in 1910, Dampier, who was a tutor of my college
when I was an undergraduate, felt no doubt that 'future ages
will see no limit to the growth of man's power over the resources of nature and of his intelligent use of them for the
welfare of his race'.[2] In view of what I am about to say, it

---

[1] Gibbon, *The Decline and Fall of the Roman Empire*, ch. xxxviii;
the occasion of this digression was the downfall of the western empire.
A critic in *The Times Literary Supplement*, November 18, 1960, quoting
this passage, asks whether Gibbon quite meant it. Of course he did;
the point of view of a writer is more likely to reflect the period in which
he lives than that about which he writes — a truth well illustrated by
this critic, who seeks to transfer his own mid-twentieth-century scepticism
to a late eighteenth-century writer.

[2] *Cambridge Modern History: Its Origin, Authorship and Production*
(1907), p. 13; *Cambridge Modern History*, i (1902), 4; xii (1910), 791.

is fair for me to admit that this was the atmosphere in which
I was educated, and that I could subscribe without reservation
to the words of my senior by half a generation, Bertrand
Russell : 'I grew up in the full flood of Victorian optimism,
and . . . something remains with me of the hopefulness that
then was easy'.[1]

In 1920, when Bury wrote his book *The Idea of Progress*,
a bleaker climate already prevailed, the blame for which he
laid, in obedience to the current fashion, on 'the doctrinaires
who have established the present reign of terror in Russia',
though he still described progress as 'the animating and con-
trolling idea of western civilization'.[2] Thereafter this note
was silent. Nicholas I of Russia is said to have issued an order
banning the word 'progress' : nowadays the philosophers and
historians of western Europe, and even the United States,
have come belatedly to agree with him. The hypothesis of
progress has been refuted. The decline of the west has become so familiar a phrase that quotation marks are no longer
required. But what, apart from all the shouting, has really
happened ? By whom has this new current of opinion been
formed ? The other day I was shocked to come across, I
think, the only remark of Bertrand Russell I have ever seen
which seemed to me to betray an acute sense of class : 'There
is, on the whole, much less liberty in the world now than there
was a hundred years ago'.[3] I have no measuring-rod for
liberty, and do not know how to balance the lesser liberty of
few against the greater liberty of many. But on any standard
of measurement I can only regard the statement as fantastically
untrue. I am more attracted by one of those fascinating
glimpses which Mr. A. J. P. Taylor sometimes gives us into
Oxford academic life. All this talk about the decline of
civilization, he writes, 'means only that university professors
used to have domestic servants and now do their own washing-

[1] B. Russell, *Portraits From Memory* (1956), p. 17.
[2] J. B. Bury, *The Idea of Progress* (1920), pp. vii-viii.
[3] B. Russell, *Portraits From Memory* (1956), p. 124.

up'.[1]   Of course, for former domestic servants, washing-up by professors may be a symbol of progress. The loss of white supremacy in Africa, which worries Empire Loyalists, Africaner Republicans and investors in gold and copper shares, may look like progress to others. I see no reason why, on this question of progress, I should *ipso facto* prefer the verdict of the 1950s to that of the 1890s, the verdict of the English-speaking world to that of Russia, Asia and Africa, or the verdict of the middle-class intellectual to that of the man in the street who, according to Mr. Macmillan, has never had it so good. Let us for the moment suspend judgment on the question whether we are living in a period of progress or of decline, and examine a little more closely what is implied in the concept of progress, what assumptions lie behind it, and how far these have become untenable.

I should like, first of all, to clear up the muddle about progress and evolution. The thinkers of the Enlightenment adopted two apparently incompatible views. They sought to vindicate man's place in the world of nature : the laws of history were equated with the laws of nature. On the other hand, they believed in progress. But what ground was there for treating nature as progressive, as constantly advancing towards a goal ? Hegel met the difficulty by sharply distinguishing history, which was progressive, from nature, which was not. The Darwinian revolution appeared to remove all embarrassments by equating evolution and progress : nature, like history, turned out after all to be progressive. But this opened the way to a much graver misunderstanding by confusing biological inheritance, which is the source of evolution, with social acquisition, which is the source of progress in history. The distinction is familiar and obvious. Put a European infant in a Chinese family, and the child will grow up with a white skin, but speaking Chinese. Pigmentation

[1] *The Observer*, June 21, 1959.

is a biological inheritance, language a social acquisition transmitted by the agency of the human brain. Evolution by inheritance has to be measured in millennia or in millions of years; no measurable biological change is known to have occurred in man since the beginning of written history. Progress by acquisition can be measured in generations. The essence of man as a rational being is that he develops his potential capacities by accumulating the experience of past generations. Modern man is said to have no larger a brain, and no greater innate capacity of thought, than his ancestor 5000 years ago. But the effectiveness of his thinking has been multiplied many times by learning and incorporating in his experience the experience of the intervening generations. The transmission of acquired characteristics, which is rejected by biologists, is the very foundation of social progress. History is progress through the transmission of acquired skills from one generation to another.

Secondly, we need not and should not conceive progress as having a finite beginning or end. The belief, popular less than fifty years ago, that civilization was invented in the Nile Valley in the fourth millennium B.C. is no more credible today than the chronology which placed the creation of the world in 4004 B.C. Civilization, the birth of which we may perhaps take as a starting-point for our hypothesis of progress, was surely not an invention, but an infinitely slow process of development, in which spectacular leaps probably occurred from time to time. We need not trouble ourselves with the question when progress—or civilization—began. The hypothesis of a finite end of progress has led to more serious misapprehension. Hegel has been rightly condemned for seeing the end of progress in the Prussian monarchy — apparently the result of an overstrained interpretation of his view of the impossibility of prediction. But Hegel's aberration was capped by that eminent Victorian, Arnold of Rugby, who in his inaugural lecture as Regius Professor of Modern History in Oxford in 1841 thought that modern history would be the last stage in the history of mankind : 'It appears to bear marks of the fullness of time, as if there would be no future history beyond it'.[1] Marx's prediction that the proletarian revolution would realize the ultimate aim of a classless society was logically and morally less vulnerable ; but the presumption of an end of history has an eschatological ring more appropriate to the theologian than to the historian, and reverts to the fallacy of a goal outside history. No doubt a finite end has attractions for the human mind ; and Acton's vision of the march of history as an unending progress towards liberty seems chilly and vague. But if the historian is to save his hypothesis of progress, I think he must be prepared to treat it as a process into which the demands and conditions of successive periods will put their own specific content. And this is what is meant by Acton's thesis that history is not only a record of progress, but a 'progressive science', or, if you like, that history in both senses of the word — as the course of events and as the record of those events — is progressive. Let us recall Acton's description of the advance of liberty in history :

> It is by the combined efforts of the weak, made under compulsion, to resist the reign of force and constant wrong, that, in the rapid change but slow progress of four hundred years, liberty has been preserved, and secured, and extended, and finally understood.[2]

History as the course of events was conceived by Acton as progress towards liberty, history as the record of those events as progress towards the understanding of liberty : the two processes advanced side by side.[3] The philosopher Bradley, writing in an age when analogies from evolution were fashionable, remarked that, 'for religious faith the end of evolution

---

[1] T. Arnold, *An Inaugural Lecture on the Study of Modern History* (1841), p. 38.
[2] Acton, *Lectures on Modern History* (1906), p. 51.
[3] K. Mannheim, *Ideology and Utopia* (Engl. transl., 1936), p. 236, also associates man's 'will to shape history' with his 'ability to understand it'.

is presented as that which . . . is already evolved'.[1] For the historian the end of progress is not already evolved. It is something still infinitely remote ; and pointers towards it come in sight only as we advance. This does not diminish its importance. A compass is a valuable and indeed indispensable guide. But it is not a chart of the route. The content of history can be realized only as we experience it.

My third point is that no sane person ever believed in a kind of progress which advanced in an unbroken straight line without reverses and deviations and breaks in continuity, so that even the sharpest reverse is not necessarily fatal to the belief. Clearly there are periods of regression as well as periods of progress. Moreover, it would be rash to assume that, after a retreat, the advance will be resumed from the same point or along the same line. Hegel's or Marx's four or three civilizations, Toynbee's twenty-one civilizations, the theory of a life-cycle of civilizations passing through rise, decline and fall — such schemes make no sense in themselves. But they are symptomatic of the observed fact that the effort which is needed to drive civilization forward dies away in one place and is later resumed at another, so that whatever progress we can observe in history is certainly not continuous either in time or in place. Indeed, if I were addicted to formulating laws of history, one such law would be to the effect that the group — call it a class, a nation, a continent, a civilization, what you will — which plays the leading role in the advance of civilization in one period is unlikely to play a similar role in the next period, and this for the good reason that it will be too deeply imbued with the traditions, interests and ideologies of the earlier period to be able to adapt itself to the demands and conditions of the next period.[2] Thus it

[1] F. H. Bradley, *Ethical Studies* (1876), p. 293.
[2] For a diagnosis of such a situation see R. S. Lynd, *Knowledge for What ?* (N.Y., 1939), p. 88 : 'Elderly people in our culture are frequently oriented towards the past, the time of their vigour and power, and resist the future as a threat. It is probable that a whole culture in an advanced stage of loss of relative power and disintegration may thus have a domi-

may very well happen that what seems for one group a period of decline may seem to another the birth of a new advance. Progress does not and cannot mean equal and simultaneous progress for all. It is significant that almost all our latter-day prophets of decline, our sceptics who see no meaning in history and assume that progress is dead, belong to that sector of the world and to that class of society which have triumphantly played a leading and predominant part in the advance of civilization for several generations. It is no consolation to them to be told that the role which their group has played in the past will now pass to others. Clearly a history which has played so scurvy a trick on them cannot be a meaningful or rational process. But, if we are to retain the hypothesis of progress, we must, I think, accept the condition of the broken line.

Lastly, I come to the question what is the essential content of progress in terms of historical action. The people who struggle, say, to extend civil rights to all, or to reform penal practice, or to remove inequalities of race or wealth are consciously seeking to do just those things : they are not consciously seeking to 'progress', to realize some historical 'law' or 'hypothesis' of progress. It is the historian who applies to their actions his hypothesis of progress, and interprets their actions as progress. But this does not invalidate the concept of progress. I am glad on this point to find myself in agreement with Sir Isaiah Berlin that 'progress and reaction, however much the words may have been abused, are not empty concepts'.[1] It is a presupposition of history that man is capable of profiting (not that he necessarily profits) by the experience of his predecessors, and that progress in history, unlike evolution in nature, rests on the transmission of acquired assets. These assets include both material possessions and the capacity to master, transform and utilize one's

nant orientation towards a lost golden age, while life is lived sluggishly along in the present.'

[1] *Foreign Affairs*, xxviii, No. 3 (June 1950), p. 382.

environment. Indeed, the two factors are closely inter-connected, and react on one another. Marx treats human labour as the foundation of the whole edifice; and this formula seems acceptable if a sufficiently broad sense is attached to 'labour'. But the mere accumulation of resources will not avail unless it brings with it not only increased technical and social knowledge and experience, but increased mastery of man's environment in the broader sense. At the present time, few people would, I think, question the fact of progress in the accumulation both of material resources and of scientific knowledge, of mastery over the environment in the technological sense. What is questioned is whether there has been in the twentieth century any progress in our ordering of society, in our mastery of the social environment, national or international, whether indeed there has not been a marked regression. Has not the evolution of man as a social being lagged fatally behind the progress of technology?

The symptoms which inspire this question are obvious. But I suspect none the less that it is wrongly put. History has known many turning-points, where the leadership and initiative has passed from one group, from one sector of the world, to another: the period of the rise of the modern state and the shift in the centre of power from the Mediterranean to western Europe, and the period of the French revolution have been conspicuous modern examples. Such periods are always times of violent upheavals and struggles for power. The old authorities weaken, the old landmarks disappear; out of a bitter clash of ambitions and resentments the new order emerges. What I would suggest is that we are now passing through such a period. It appears to me simply untrue to say that our understanding of the problems of social organization or our good will to organize society in the light of that understanding have regressed: indeed, I should venture to say that they have greatly increased. It is not that our capacities have diminished, or our moral qualities declined. But the period of conflict and upheaval, due to the shifting balance of power between continents, nations and classes, through which we are living, has enormously increased the strain on these capacities and qualities, and limited and frustrated their effectiveness for positive achievement. While I do not wish to underestimate the force of the challenge of the past fifty years to the belief in progress in the western world, I am still not convinced that progress in history has come to an end. But, if you press me further on the content of progress, I think I can only reply something like this. The notion of a finite and clearly definable goal of progress in history, so often postulated by nineteenth-century thinkers, has proved inapplicable and barren. Belief in progress means belief not in any automatic or inevitable process, but in the progressive development of human potentialities. Progress is an abstract term ; and the concrete ends pursued by mankind arise from time to time out of the course of history, not from some source outside it. I profess no belief in the perfectibility of man, or in a future paradise on earth. To this extent I would agree with the theologians and the mystics who assert that perfection is not realizable in history. But I shall be content with the possibility of unlimited progress — or progress subject to no limits that we can or need envisage — towards goals which can be defined only as we advance towards them, and the validity of which can be verified only in a process of attaining them. Nor do I know how, without some such conception of progress, society can survive. Every civilized society imposes sacrifices on the living generation for the sake of generations yet unborn. To justify these sacrifices in the name of a better world in the future is the secular counterpart of justifying them in the name of some divine purpose. In Bury's words, 'the principle of duty to posterity is a direct corollary of the idea of progress'.[1] Perhaps this duty does not require justification. If it does, I know of no other way to justify it.

[1] J. B. Bury, *The Idea of Progress* (1920), p. ix.

This brings me to the famous crux of objectivity in history. The word itself is misleading and question-begging. In an earlier lecture I have already argued that the social sciences — and history among them — cannot accommodate themselves to a theory of knowledge which puts subject and object asunder, and enforces a rigid separation between the observer and the thing observed. We need a new model which does justice to the complex process of interrelation and interaction between them. The facts of history cannot be purely objective, since they become facts of history only in virtue of the significance attached to them by the historian. Objectivity in history — if we are still to use the conventional term — cannot be an objectivity of fact, but only of relation, of the relation between fact and interpretation, between past, present and future. I need not revert to the reasons which led me to reject as unhistorical the attempt to judge historical events by erecting an absolute standard of value outside history and independent of it. But the concept of absolute truth is also not appropriate to the world of history — or, I suspect, to the world of science. It is only the simplest kind of historical statement that can be adjudged absolutely true or absolutely false. At a more sophisticated level, the historian who contests, say, the verdict of one of his predecessors will normally condemn it, not as absolutely false, but as inadequate or one-sided or misleading, or the product of a point of view which has been rendered obsolete or irrelevant by later evidence. To say that the Russian revolution was due to the stupidity of Nicholas II or to the genius of Lenin is altogether inadequate — so inadequate as to be altogether misleading. But it cannot be called absolutely false. The historian does not deal in absolutes of this kind.

Let us go back to the sad case of Robinson's death. The objectivity of our enquiry into that event depended not on getting our facts right — these were not in dispute — but on distinguishing between the real or significant facts, in which we were interested, and the accidental facts, which we could afford to ignore. We found it easy to draw this distinction because our standard or test of significance, the basis of our objectivity, was clear, and consisted of relevance to the goal in view, *i.e.* reduction of deaths on the roads. But the historian is a less fortunate person than the investigator who has before him the simple and finite purpose of reducing traffic casualties. The historian, too, in his task of interpretation, needs his standard of significance, which is also his standard of objectivity, in order to distinguish between the significant and the accidental; and he too can find it only in relevance to the end in view. But this is necessarily an evolving end, since the evolving interpretation of the past is a necessary function of history. The traditional assumption that change has always to be explained in terms of something fixed and unchangeable is contrary to the experience of the historian. 'For the historian', says Professor Butterfield, perhaps implicitly reserving for himself a sphere into which historians need not follow him, 'the only absolute is change'.[1] The absolute in history is not something in the past from which we start; it is not something in the present, since all present thinking is necessarily relative. It is something still incomplete and in process of becoming — something in the future towards which we move, which begins to take shape only as we move towards it, and in the light of which, as we move forward, we gradually shape our interpretation of the past. This is the secular truth behind the religious myth that the meaning of history will be revealed in the Day of Judgment. Our criterion is not an absolute in the static sense of something that is the same yesterday, today and for ever: such an absolute

[1] H. Butterfield, *The Whig Interpretation of History* (1931), p. 58; compare the more elaborate statement in A. von Martin, *The Sociology of the Renaissance* (Engl. trans., 1945), p. i: 'Inertia and motion, static and dynamic, are fundamental categories with which to begin a sociological approach to history. . . . History knows inertia in a relative sense only: the decisive question is whether inertia or change predominates.' Change is the positive and absolute, inertia the subjective and relative, element in history.

is incompatible with the nature of history. But it is an absolute in respect of our interpretation of the past. It rejects the relativist view that one interpretation is as good as another, or that every interpretation is true in its own time and place, and it provides the touchstone by which our interpretation of the past will ultimately be judged. It is this sense of direction in history which alone enables us to order and interpret the events of the past — the task of the historian — and to liberate and organize human energies in the present with a view to the future — the task of the statesman, the economist and the social reformer. But the process itself remains progressive and dynamic. Our sense of direction, and our interpretation of the past, are subject to constant modification and evolution as we proceed.

Hegel clothed his absolute in the mystical shape of a world spirit, and made the cardinal error of bringing the course of history to an end in the present instead of projecting it into the future. He recognized a process of continuous evolution in the past, and incongruously denied it in the future. Those who, since Hegel, have reflected most deeply on the nature of history have seen in it a synthesis of past and future. Tocqueville, who did not entirely free himself from the theological idiom of his day and gave too narrow content to his absolute, nevertheless had the essence of the matter. Having spoken of the development of equality as a universal and permanent phenomenon, he went on :

> If the men of our time were brought to see the gradual and progressive development of equality as at once the past and the future of their history, this single discovery would give that development the sacred character of the will of their lord and master.[1]

An important chapter of history could be written on that still unfinished theme. Marx, who shared some of Hegel's inhibitions about looking into the future, and was principally con-

---

[1] De Tocqueville, Preface to *Democracy in America*.

cerned to root his teaching firmly in past history, was compelled by the nature of his theme to project into the future his absolute of the classless society. Bury described the idea of progress, a little awkwardly, but clearly with the same intention, as 'a theory which involves a synthesis of the past and a prophecy of the future'.[1] Historians, says Namier in a deliberately paradoxical phrase, which he proceeds to illustrate with his usual wealth of examples, 'imagine the past and remember the future'.[2] Only the future can provide the key to the interpretation of the past; and it is only in this sense that we can speak of an ultimate objectivity in history. It is at once the justification and the explanation of history that the past throws light on the future, and the future throws light on the past.

What, then, do we mean when we praise a historian for being objective, or say that one historian is more objective than another? Not, it is clear, simply that he gets his facts right, but rather that he chooses the right facts, or, in other words, that he applies the right standard of significance. When we call a historian objective, we mean I think two things. First of all, we mean that he has a capacity to rise above the limited vision of his own situation in society and in history — a capacity which, as I suggested in an earlier lecture, is partly dependent on his capacity to recognize the extent of his involvement in that situation, to recognize, that is to say, the impossibility of total objectivity. Secondly, we mean that he has the capacity to project his vision into the future in such a way as to give him a more profound and more lasting insight into the past than can be attained by those historians whose outlook is entirely bounded by their own immediate situation. No historian today will echo Acton's confidence in the prospect of 'ultimate history'. But some historians write history which is more durable, and has more of this ultimate and objective character, than others; and

[1] J. B. Bury, *The Idea of Progress* (1920), p. 5.
[2] L. B. Namier, *Conflicts* (1942), p. 70.

these are the historians who have what I may call a long-term vision over the past and over the future. The historian of the past can make an approach towards objectivity only as he approaches towards the understanding of the future.

When, therefore, I spoke of history in an earlier lecture as a dialogue between past and present, I should rather have called it a dialogue between the events of the past and progressively emerging future ends. The historian's interpretation of the past, his selection of the significant and the relevant, evolves with the progressive emergence of new goals. To take the simplest of all illustrations, so long as the main goal appeared to be the organization of constitutional liberties and political rights, the historian interpreted the past in constitutional and political terms. When economic and social ends began to replace constitutional and political ends, historians turned to economic and social interpretations of the past. In this process, the sceptic might plausibly allege that the new interpretation is no truer than the old; each is true for its period. Nevertheless, since the preoccupation with economic and social ends represents a broader and more advanced stage in human development than the preoccupation with political and constitutional ends, so the economic and social interpretation of history may be said to represent a more advanced stage in history than the exclusively political interpretation. The old interpretation is not rejected, but is both included and superseded in the new. Historiography is a progressive science in the sense that it seeks to provide constantly expanding and deepening insights into a course of events which is itself progressive. This is what I should mean by saying that we need 'a constructive outlook over the past'. Modern historiography has grown up during the past two centuries in this dual belief in progress, and cannot survive without it, since it is this belief which provides it with its standard of significance, its touchstone for distinguishing between the real and the accidental. Goethe, in a conversation towards the end of his life, cut the Gordian knot a little brusquely :

When eras are on the decline, all tendencies are subjective ; but on the other hand when matters are ripening for a new epoch, all tendencies are objective.[1]

Nobody is obliged to believe either in the future of history or in the future of society. It is possible that our society may be destroyed or may perish of slow decay, and that history may relapse into theology — that is to say, a study not of human achievement, but of the divine purpose — or into literature — that is to say, a telling of stories and legends without purpose or significance. But this will not be history in the sense in which we have known it in the last 200 years.

I have still to deal with the familiar and popular objection to any theory which finds the ultimate criterion of historical judgment in the future. Such a theory, it is said, implies that success is the ultimate criterion of judgment, and that, if not whatever is, whatever will be, is right. For the past 200 years most historians have not only assumed a direction in which history is moving, but have consciously or unconsciously believed that this direction was on the whole the right direction, that mankind was moving from the worse to the better, from the lower to the higher. The historian not only recognized the direction, but endorsed it. The test of significance which he applied in his approach to the past was not only a sense of the course on which history was moving, but a sense of his own moral involvement in that course. The alleged dichotomy between the 'is' and the 'ought', between fact and value, was resolved. It was an optimistic view, a product of an age of overwhelming confidence in the future ; Whigs and Liberals, Hegelians and Marxists, theologians and rationalists, remained firmly, and more or less articulately, committed to it. For 200 years it could have been described without much exaggeration as the accepted

[1] Quoted in J. Huizinga, *Men and Ideas* (1959), p. 50.

and implicit answer to the question, What is History ? The reaction against it has come with the current mood of apprehension and pessimism, which has left the field clear for the theologians who seek the meaning of history outside history, and for the sceptics who find no meaning in history at all. We are assured on all hands, and with the utmost emphasis, that the dichotomy between 'is' and 'ought' is absolute and cannot be resolved, that 'values' cannot be derived from 'facts'. This is, I think, a false trail. Let us see how a few historians, or writers about history, chosen more or less at random, have felt about this question.

Gibbon justifies the amount of space devoted in his narrative to the victories of Islam on the ground that 'the disciples of Mohammed still hold the civil and religious sceptre of the Oriental world'. But, he adds, 'the same labour would be unworthily bestowed on the swarms of savages who, between the 7th and 12th centuries, descended from the plains of Scythia', since 'the majesty of the Byzantine throne repelled and survived these disorderly attacks'.[1] This seems not unreasonable. History is, by and large, a record of what people did, not of what they failed to do : to this extent it is inevitably a success story. Professor Tawney remarks that historians give 'an appearance of inevitableness' to an existing order 'by dragging into prominence the forces which have triumphed and thrusting into the background those which they have swallowed up'.[2] But is not this in a sense the essence of the historian's job ? The historian must not underestimate the opposition ; he must not represent the victory as a walkover if it was touch-and-go. Sometimes those who were defeated have made as great a contribution to the ultimate result as the victors. These are familiar maxims to every historian. But, by and large, the historian is concerned with those who, whether victorious or defeated, achieved some-

[1] Gibbon, *The Decline and Fall of the Roman Empire*, ch. lv.
[2] R. H. Tawney, *The Agrarian Problem in the Sixteenth Century* (1912), p. 177.

thing. I am not a specialist in the history of cricket. But its pages are presumably studded with the names of those who made centuries rather than of those who made ducks and were left out of the side. Hegel's famous statement that in history 'only those peoples can come under our notice which form a state',[1] has been justly criticized as attaching an exclusive value to one form of social organization and paving the way for an obnoxious state-worship. But, in principle, what Hegel is trying to say is correct, and reflects the familiar distinction between pre-history and history; only those peoples which have succeeded in organizing their society in some degree cease to be primitive savages and enter into history. Carlyle, in his *French Revolution* called Louis XV 'a very World Solecism incarnate'. He evidently liked the phrase, for he embroidered it later in a longer passage :

> What new universal vertiginous movement is this : of institutions, social arrangements, individual minds, which once worked cooperative, now rolling and grinding in distracted collision ? Inevitable ; it is the breaking-up of a World Solecism, worn out at last.[2]

The criterion is once more historical : what fitted one epoch had become a solecism in another, and is condemned on that account. Even Sir Isaiah Berlin, when he descends from the heights of philosophical abstraction and considers concrete historical situations, appears to have come round to this view. In a broadcast delivered some time after the publication of his essay on *Historical Inevitability*, he praised Bismarck, in spite of moral shortcomings, as a 'genius' and 'the greatest example in the last century of a politician of the highest powers of political judgment', and contrasted him favourably in this respect with such men as Joseph II of Austria, Robespierre, Lenin and Hitler who failed to realize 'their positive ends'. I find this verdict odd. But what interests me at the

---

[1] *Lectures on the Philosophy of History* (English transl., 1884), p. 40.
[2] T. Carlyle, *The French Revolution*, I, i, ch. 4 ; I, iii, ch. 7.

moment is the criterion of judgment. Bismarck, says Sir Isaiah, understood the material in which he was working; the others were led away by abstract theories which failed to work. The moral is that 'failure comes from resisting that which works best . . . in favour of some systematic method or principle claiming universal validity'.[1] In other words the criterion of judgment in history is not some 'principle claiming universal validity', but 'that which works best'.

It is not only — I need hardly say — when analysing the past that we invoke this criterion of 'what works best'. If someone informed you that he thought that, at the present juncture, the union of Great Britain and the United States of America in a single state under a single sovereignty was desirable, you might agree that this was quite a sensible view. If he went on to say that constitutional monarchy was preferable to presidential democracy as a form of government, you might also agree that this was quite sensible. But suppose he then told you that he proposed to devote himself to conducting a campaign for the reunion of the two countries under the British crown; you would probably reply that he would be wasting his time. If you tried to explain why, you would have to tell him that issues of this kind have to be debated on the basis not of some principle of general application, but of what would work in given historical conditions; you might even commit the cardinal sin of speaking of history with a capital H and tell him that History was against him. The business of the politician is to consider not merely what is morally or theoretically desirable, but also the forces which exist in the world, and how they can be directed or manipulated to probably partial realizations of the ends in view. Our political decisions taken in the light of our interpretation of history are rooted in this compromise. But our interpretation of history is rooted in the same compromise. Nothing is more radically false than to set up some supposedly abstract

[1] Broadcast on 'Political Judgment' in the Third Programme of the B.B.C., June 19, 1957.

standard of the desirable and condemn the past in the light of it. For the word 'success', which has come to have invidious connotations, let us by all means substitute the neutral 'that which works best'. Since I have joined issue with Sir Isaiah Berlin on several occasions during these lectures, I am glad to be able to close the account with, at any rate, this measure of agreement.

But acceptance of the criterion of 'what works best' does not make its application either easy or self-evident. It is not a criterion which encourages snap verdicts, or which bows down to the view that what is, is right. Pregnant failures are not unknown in history. History recognizes what I may call 'delayed achievement': the apparent failures of today may turn out to have made a vital contribution to the achievement of tomorrow — prophets born before their time. Indeed, one of the advantages of this criterion over the criterion of a supposedly fixed and universal principle is that it may require us to postpone our judgment or to qualify it in the light of things that have not yet happened. Proudhon, who talked freely in terms of abstract moral principles, condoned the *coup d'état* of Napoleon III after it had succeeded; Marx, who rejected the criterion of abstract moral principles, condemned Proudhon for condoning it. Looking back from a longer historical perspective, we shall probably agree that Proudhon was wrong and Marx right. The achievement of Bismarck provides an excellent starting-point for an examination of this problem of historical judgment; and, while I accept Sir Isaiah's criterion of 'what works best', I am still puzzled by the narrow and short-term limits within which he is apparently content to apply it. Did what Bismarck created really work well? I should have thought that it led to an immense disaster. This does not mean that I am seeking to condemn Bismarck who created the German Reich, or the mass of Germans who wanted it and helped to create it. But, as a historian, I still have many questions to ask. Did the eventual disaster occur because some hidden flaws existed in the structure of the Reich? or because something in the internal conditions which brought it to birth destined it to become self-assertive and aggressive? or because, when the Reich was created, the European or world scene was already so crowded, and expansive tendencies among the existing Great Powers already so strong, that the emergence of another expansive Great Power was sufficient to cause a major collision and bring down the whole system in ruins? On the last hypothesis, it may be wrong to hold Bismarck and the German people responsible, or solely responsible, for the disaster: you cannot really blame the last straw. But an objective judgment on Bismarck's achievement and how it worked awaits an answer from the historian to these questions, and I am not sure that he is yet in a position to answer them all definitively. What I would say is that the historian of the 1920s was nearer to objective judgment than the historian of the 1880s, and that the historian of today is nearer than the historian of the 1920s; the historian of the year 2000 may be nearer still. This illustrates my thesis that objectivity in history does not and cannot rest on some fixed and immovable standard of judgment existing here and now, but only on a standard which is laid up in the future and is evolved as the course of history advances. History acquires meaning and objectivity only when it establishes a coherent relation between past and future.

Let us now take another look at this alleged dichotomy between fact and value. Values cannot be derived from facts. This statement is partly true, but partly false. You have only to examine the system of values prevailing in any period or in any country to realize how much of it is moulded by the facts of the environment. In an earlier lecture I drew attention to the changing historical content of value-words like liberty, equality or justice. Or take the Christian church as an institution largely concerned with the propagation of moral values. Contrast the values of primitive Christianity with those of the mediaeval papacy, or the values of the mediaeval papacy with those of the Protestant churches of the nineteenth century. Or contrast the values promulgated today by, say, the Christian church in Spain with the values promulgated by the Christian churches in the United States. These differences in values spring from differences of historical fact. Or consider the historical facts which in the last century and a half have caused slavery or racial inequality or the exploitation of child labour — all once accepted as morally neutral or reputable — to be generally regarded as immoral. The proposition that values cannot be derived from facts is, to say the least, one-sided and misleading. Or let us reverse the statement. Facts cannot be derived from values. This is partly true, but may also be misleading, and requires qualification. When we seek to know the facts, the questions which we ask, and therefore the answers which we obtain, are prompted by our system of values. Our picture of the facts of our environment is moulded by our values, *i.e.* by the categories through which we approach the facts ; and this picture is one of the important facts of which we have to take into account. Values enter into the facts and are an essential part of them. Our values are an essential part of our equipment as human beings. It is through our values that we have that capacity to adapt ourselves to our environment, and to adapt our environment to ourselves, to acquire that mastery over our environment, which has made history a record of progress. But do not, in dramatizing the struggle of man with his environment, set up a false antithesis and a false separation between facts and values. Progress in history is achieved through the interdependence and interaction of facts and values. The objective historian is the historian who penetrates most deeply into this reciprocal process.

A clue to this problem of facts and values is provided by our ordinary use of the word 'truth' — a word which straddles the world of fact and the world of value and is made up of elements of both. Nor is this an idiosyncrasy of the English language. The words for truth in the Latin languages, the German *Wahrheit*, the Russian *pravda*,[1] all possess this dual character. Every language appears to require this word for a truth which is not merely a statement of fact and not merely a value judgment, but embraces both elements. It may be a fact that I went to London last week. But you would not ordinarily call it a truth : it is devoid of any value content. On the other hand, when the Founding Fathers of the United States in the Declaration of Independence referred to the self-evident truth that all men are created equal, you may feel that the value content of the statement predominates over the factual content, and may on that account challenge its right to be regarded as a truth. Somewhere between these two poles — the north pole of valueless facts and the south pole of value judgments still struggling to transform themselves into facts — lies the realm of historical truth. The historian, as I said in my first lecture, is balanced between fact and interpretation, between fact and value. He cannot separate them. It may be that, in a static world, you are obliged to pronounce a divorce between fact and value. But history is meaningless in a static world. History in its essence is change, movement or — if you do not cavil at the old-fashioned word — progress.

I return therefore in conclusion to Acton's description of progress as 'the scientific hypothesis on which history is to be written'. You can, if you please, turn history into theology by making the meaning of the past depend on some extra-historical and super-rational power. You can, if you please, turn it into literature — a collection of stories and legends about the past without meaning or significance. History properly so-called can be written only by those who find and accept a sense of direction in history itself. The belief that we have come from somewhere is closely linked with the belief

---

[1] The case of *pravda* is especially interesting since there is another old Russian word for truth, *istina*. But the distinction is not between truth as fact and truth as value ; *pravda* is human truth in both aspects, *istina* divine truth in both aspects — truth about God and truth as revealed by God.

that we are going somewhere. A society which has lost belief in its capacity to progress in the future will quickly cease to concern itself with its progress in the past. As I said at the beginning of my first lecture, our view of history reflects our view of society. I now come back to my starting-point by declaring my faith in the future of society and in the future of history.

# VI

## *The Widening Horizon*

THE conception which I have put forward in these lectures of history as a constantly moving process, with the historian moving within it, seems to commit me to some concluding reflexions on the position of history and of the historian in our time. We live in an epoch when — not for the first time in history — predictions of world catastrophe are in the air, and weigh heavily on all. They can be neither proved nor disproved. But they are at any rate far less certain than the prediction that we shall all die; and, since the certainty of that prediction does not prevent us from laying plans for our own future, so I shall proceed to discuss the present and future of our society on the assumption that this country — or, if not this country, some major part of the world — will survive the hazards that threaten us, and that history will continue.

The middle years of the twentieth century find the world in a process of change probably more profound and more sweeping than any which has overtaken it since the mediaeval world broke up in ruins and the foundations of the modern world were laid in the fifteenth and sixteenth centuries. The change is no doubt ultimately the product of scientific discoveries and inventions, of their ever more widespread application, and of developments arising directly or indirectly out of them. The most conspicuous aspect of the change is a social revolution comparable with that which, in the fifteenth and sixteenth centuries, inaugurated the rise to power of a new class based on finance and commerce, and later on industry. The new structure of our industry and the new structure of our society present problems too vast for me to embark on here. But the change has two aspects more immediately relevant to my theme — what I may call a change in depth, and a change in geographical extent. I will attempt to touch briefly on both of these.

History begins when men begin to think of the passage of time in terms not of natural processes — the cycle of the seasons, the human life-span — but of a series of specific events in which men are consciously involved and which they can consciously influence. History, says Burckhardt, is 'the break with nature caused by the awakening of consciousness'.[1] History is the long struggle of man, by the exercise of his reason, to understand his environment and to act upon it. But the modern period has broadened the struggle in a revolutionary way. Man now seeks to understand, and to act on, not only his environment, but himself; and this has added, so to speak, a new dimension to reason, and a new dimension to history. The present age is the most historically minded of all ages. Modern man is to an unprecedented degree self-conscious and therefore conscious of history. He peers eagerly back into the twilight out of which he has come in the hope that its faint beams will illuminate the obscurity into which he is going; and, conversely, his aspirations and anxieties about the path that lies ahead quicken his insight into what lies behind. Past, present and future are linked together in the endless chain of history.

The change in the modern world which consisted in the development of man's consciousness of himself may be said to begin with Descartes, who first established man's position as a being who can not only think, but think about his own thinking, who can observe himself in the act of observing, so that man is simultaneously the subject and the object of thought and observation. But the development did not become fully

[1] J. Burckhardt, *Reflections on History* (1959), p. 31.

explicit till the latter part of the eighteenth century, when Rousseau opened up new depths of human self-understanding and self-consciousness, and gave man a new outlook on the world of nature and on traditional civilization. The French revolution, said Tocqueville, was inspired by 'the belief that what was wanted was to replace the complex of traditional customs governing the social order of the day by simple, elementary rules deriving from the exercise of the human reason and from natural law'.[1] 'Never till then', wrote Acton in one of his manuscript notes, 'had men sought liberty, knowing what they sought';[2] for Acton, as for Hegel, liberty and reason were never far apart. And with the French revolution was linked the American revolution.

> Four score and seven years ago our fathers brought forth upon this continent a new nation, conceived in liberty, and dedicated to the proposition that all men are created equal.

It was, as Lincoln's words suggest, a unique event — the first occasion in history when men deliberately and consciously formed themselves into a nation, and then consciously and deliberately set out to mould other men into it. In the seventeenth and eighteenth centuries man had already become fully conscious of the world around him and of its laws. They were no longer the mysterious decrees of an inscrutable providence, but laws accessible to reason. But they were laws to which man was subject, and not laws of his own making. In the next stage man was to become fully conscious of his power over his environment and over himself and of his right to make the laws under which he would live.

The transition from the eighteenth century to the modern world was long and gradual. Its representative philosophers were Hegel and Marx, both of whom occupy an ambivalent position. Hegel is rooted in the idea of laws of providence

---

[1] A. de Tocqueville, *De l'Ancien Régime*, III, ch. 1.
[2] Cambridge University Library : Add. MSS. 4870.

converted into laws of reason. Hegel's world spirit grasps providence firmly with one hand and reason with the other. He echoes Adam Smith. Individuals 'gratify their own interests ; but something more is thereby accomplished which is latent in their action though not present in their consciousness'. Of the rational purpose of the world spirit he writes that men, 'in the very act of realizing it, make it the occasion of satisfying their desire, whose import is different from that purpose'. This is simply the harmony of interests translated into the language of German philosophy.[1] Hegel's equivalent for Smith's 'hidden hand' was the famous 'cunning of reason' which sets men to work to fulfil purposes of which they are not conscious. But Hegel was none the less the philosopher of the French revolution, the first philosopher to see the essence of reality in historical change and in the development of man's consciousness of himself. Development in history meant development towards the concept of freedom. But, after 1815, the inspiration of the French revolution fizzled out in the doldrums of the Restoration. Hegel was politically too timid and, in his later years, too firmly entrenched in the Establishment of his day to introduce any concrete meaning into his metaphysical propositions. Herzen's description of Hegel's doctrines as 'the algebra of revolution' was singularly apt. Hegel provided the notation, but gave it no practical content. It was left for Marx to write the arithmetic into Hegel's algebraical equations.

A disciple both of Adam Smith and of Hegel, Marx started from the conception of a world ordered by rational laws of nature. Like Hegel, but this time in a practical and concrete form, he made the transition to the conception of a world ordered by laws evolving through a rational process in response to man's revolutionary initiative. In Marx's final synthesis history meant three things, which were inseparable one from another and formed a coherent and rational whole : the motion of events in accordance with objective, and

[1] The quotations are from Hegel's *Philosophy of History*.

primarily economic, laws ; the corresponding development of thought through a dialectical process ; and corresponding action in the form of the class struggle which reconciles and unites the theory and practice of revolution. What Marx offers is a synthesis of objective laws and of conscious action to translate them into practice, of what are sometimes (though misleadingly) called determinism and voluntarism. Marx constantly writes of laws to which men have hitherto been subject without being conscious of them : he more than once drew attention to what he called the 'false consciousness' of those enmeshed in a capitalist economy and capitalist society : 'the conceptions formed about the laws of production in the minds of the agents of production and circulation will differ widely from the real laws'.[1] But one finds in Marx's writings striking examples of calls for conscious revolutionary action. 'Philosophers have only interpreted the world differently', ran the famous thesis on Feuerbach ; 'but the point is to change it.' 'The proletariat', declared the *Communist Manifesto*, 'will use its political dominance to strip the bourgeoisie step by step of all capital, and concentrate all means of production in the hands of the state.' And in *The Eighteenth Brumaire of Louis Bonaparte*, Marx spoke of 'intellectual self-consciousness dissolving by a century-old process all traditional ideas'. It was the proletariat which would dissolve the false consciousness of capitalist society, and introduce the true consciousness of the classless society. But the failure of the revolutions of 1848 was a serious and dramatic set-back to developments which had seemed imminent when Marx began to work. The latter part of the nineteenth century passed in an atmosphere which was still predominantly one of prosperity and security. It was not till the turn of the century that we complete the transition to the contemporary period of history, in which the primary function of reason is no longer to understand objective laws governing the behaviour of man in society, but rather to re-shape society and the individuals who com-

[1] *Capital*, iii (Engl. transl., 1909), 369.

pose it by conscious action. In Marx, 'class', though not precisely defined, remains on the whole an objective conception to be established by economic analysis. In Lenin, the emphasis shifts from 'class' to 'party', which constitutes the vanguard of the class and infuses into it the necessary element of class-consciousness. In Marx, 'ideology' is a negative term — a product of the false consciousness of the capitalist order of society. In Lenin, 'ideology' becomes neutral or positive — a belief implanted by an élite of class-conscious leaders in a mass of potentially class-conscious workers. The moulding of class-consciousness is no longer an automatic process, but a job to be undertaken.

The other great thinker who has added a fresh dimension to reason in our time is Freud. Freud remains today a somewhat enigmatic figure. He was by training and background a nineteenth-century liberal individualist, and accepted without question the common, but misleading, assumption of a fundamental antithesis between the individual and society. Freud, approaching man as a biological rather than as a social entity, tended to treat the social environment as something historically given rather than as something in constant process of creation and transformation by man himself. He has always been attacked by the Marxists for approaching what are really social problems from the standpoint of the individual, and condemned as a reactionary on that account; and this charge, which was valid only in part against Freud himself, has been much more fully justified by the current neo-Freudian school in the United States, which assumes that maladjustments are inherent in the individual and not in the structure of society, and treats the adaptation of the individual to society as the essential function of psychology. The other popular charge against Freud, that he has extended the role of the irrational in human affairs, is totally false, and rests on a crude confusion between recognition of the irrational element in human behaviour and a cult of the irrational. That a cult of the irrational does exist in the English-speaking world today, mainly in the form of a depreciation of the achievements and potentialities of reason, is unfortunately true; it is part of the current wave of pessimism and ultra-conservatism, of which I will speak later. But this does not stem from Freud, who was an unqualified and rather primitive rationalist. What Freud did was to extend the range of our knowledge and understanding by opening up the unconscious roots of human behaviour to consciousness and to rational enquiry. This was an extension of the domain of reason, an increase in man's power to understand and control himself, and therefore his environment; and it represents a revolutionary and progressive achievement. In this respect, Freud complements, and does not contradict, the work of Marx. Freud belongs to the contemporary world in the sense that, though he himself did not entirely escape from the conception of a fixed and invariable human nature, he provided tools for a deeper understanding of the roots of human behaviour and thus for its conscious modification through rational processes.

For the historian Freud's special significance is twofold. In the first place, Freud has driven the last nail into the coffin of the ancient illusion that the motives from which men allege or believe themselves to have acted are in fact adequate to explain their action: this is a negative achievement of some importance, though the positive claim of some enthusiasts to throw light on the behaviour of the great men of history by the methods of psycho-analysis should be taken with a pinch of salt. The procedure of psycho-analysis rests on the cross-examination of the patient who is being investigated: you cannot cross-examine the dead. Secondly, Freud, reinforcing the work of Marx, has encouraged the historian to examine himself and his own position in history, the motives — perhaps hidden motives — which have guided his choice of theme or period and his selection and interpretation of the facts, the national and social background which has determined his angle of vision, the conception of the future which shapes his conception of the past. Since Marx and Freud wrote, the historian has no excuse to think of himself as a detached individual standing outside society and outside history. This is the age of self-consciousness: the historian can and should know what he is doing.

This transition to what I have called the contemporary world — the extension to new spheres of the function and power of reason — is not yet complete: it is part of the revolutionary change through which the twentieth-century world is passing. I should like to examine some of the main symptoms of the transition.

Let me begin with economics. Down to 1914 belief in objective economic laws, which governed the economic behaviour of men and nations, and which they could defy only to their own detriment, was still virtually unchallenged. Trade cycles, price fluctuations, unemployment, were determined by those laws. As late as 1930, when the great depression set in, this was still the dominant view. Thereafter things moved fast. In the 1930s, people began to talk of 'the end of economic man', meaning the man who consistently pursued his economic interests in accordance with economic laws; and since then nobody, except a few Rip Van Winkles of the nineteenth century, believes in economic laws in this sense. Today economics has become either a series of theoretical mathematical equations, or a practical study of how some people push others around. The change is mainly a product of the transition from individual to large-scale capitalism. So long as the individual entrepreneur and merchant predominated, nobody seemed in control of the economy or capable of influencing it in any significant way; and the illusion of impersonal laws and processes was preserved. Even the Bank of England, in the days of its greatest power, was thought of not as a skilful operator and manipulator, but as an objective and quasi-automatic registrar of economic trends. But with the transition from a *laissez-faire* economy to a managed economy (whether a managed capitalist economy or a socialist economy, whether the management is done by

large-scale capitalist, and nominally private, concerns or by
the state), this illusion is dissolved. It becomes clear that
certain people are taking certain decisions for certain ends;
and that these decisions set our economic course for us.
Everyone knows today that the price of oil or soap does not
vary in response to some objective law of supply and demand.
Everyone knows, or thinks he knows, that slumps and unemployment are man-made: governments admit, indeed
claim, that they know how to cure them. The transition has
been made from *laissez-faire* to planning, from the unconscious
to the self-conscious, from belief in objective economic laws
to belief that man by his own action can be the master of his
economic destiny. Social policy has gone hand in hand with
economic policy: indeed economic policy has been incorpor-
ated in social policy. Let me quote from the last volume of
the first *Cambridge Modern History*, published in 1910, a
highly perceptive comment from a writer who was anything but a Marxist and had probably never heard of
Lenin:

> The belief in the possibility of social reform by con-
> scious effort is the dominant current of the European
> mind; it has superseded the belief in liberty as the one
> panacea. . . . Its currency in the present is as significant
> and as pregnant as the belief in the rights of man about
> the time of the French revolution.[1]

Today, fifty years after this passage was written, more than
forty years after the Russian revolution, and thirty years after
the great depression, this belief has become a commonplace;
and the transition from submission to objective economic
laws which, though supposedly rational, were beyond man's
control to belief in the capacity of man to control his economic
destiny by conscious action seems to me to represent an ad-

[1] *Cambridge Modern History*, xii (1910), 15; the author of the
chapter was S. Leathes, one of the editors of the *History*, and a Civil
Service Commissioner.

vance in the application of reason to human affairs, an increased capacity in man to understand and master himself and his environment, which I should be prepared, if necessary, to call by the old-fashioned name of progress.

I have no space to touch in detail on the similar processes at work in other fields. Even science, as we have seen, is now less concerned to investigate and establish objective laws of nature, than to frame working hypotheses by which man may be enabled to harness nature to his purposes and transform his environment. More significant, man has begun, through the conscious exercise of reason, not only to transform his environment but to transform himself. At the end of the eighteenth century Malthus, in an epoch-making work, attempted to establish objective laws of population working, like Adam Smith's laws of the market, without anyone being conscious of the process. Today nobody believes in such objective laws; but the control of population has become a matter of rational and conscious social policy. We have seen in our time the lengthening by human effort of the span of human life and the altering of the balance between the generations in our population. We have heard of drugs consciously used to influence human behaviour, and surgical operations designed to alter human character. Both man and society have changed, and have been changed by conscious human effort, before our eyes. But the most significant of these changes have probably been those brought about by the development and use of modern methods of persuasion and indoctrination. Educators at all levels are nowadays more and more consciously concerned to make their contribution to the shaping of society in a particular mould, and to inculcate in the rising generation the attitudes, loyalties and opinions appropriate to that type of society; educational policy is an integral part of any rationally planned social policy. The primary function of reason, as applied to man in society, is no longer merely to investigate, but to transform; and this heightened consciousness of the power of man to improve the management of his social, economic and political affairs by the application of rational processes seems to me one of the major aspects of the twentieth-century revolution.

This expansion of reason is merely part of the process which I called in an earlier lecture 'individualization' — the diversification of individual skills and occupations and opportunities which is the concomitant of an advancing civilization. Perhaps the most far-reaching social consequence of the industrial revolution has been the progressive increase in the numbers of those who learn to think, to use their reason. In Great Britain our passion for gradualism is such that the movement is sometimes scarcely perceptible. We have rested on the laurels of universal elementary education for the best part of a century, and have still not advanced very far or very quickly towards universal higher education. This did not matter so much when we led the world. It matters more when we are being overtaken by others in a greater hurry than ourselves, and when the pace has everywhere been speeded up by technological change. For the social revolution and the technological revolution and the scientific revolution are part and parcel of the same process. If you want an academic example of the process of individualization, consider the immense diversification over the past fifty or sixty years of history, or of science, or of any particular science, and the enormously increased variety of individual specializations which it offers. But I have a far more striking example of the process at a different level. More than thirty years ago a high German military officer visiting the Soviet Union listened to some illuminating remarks from a Soviet officer concerned with the building up of the Red air force:

> We Russians have to do with still primitive human material. We are compelled to adapt the flying machine to the type of flyer who is at our disposal. To the extent to which we are successful in developing a new type of men, the technical development of the material will also

be perfected. The two factors condition each other. Primitive men cannot be put into complicated machines.[1]

Today, a bare generation later, we know that Russian machines are no longer primitive, and that millions of Russian men and women who plan, build and operate these machines are no longer primitive either. As a historian, I am more interested in this latter phenomenon. The rationalization of production means something far more important — the rationalization of man. All over the world today primitive men are learning to use complicated machines, and in doing so are learning to think, to use their reason. The revolution, which you may justly call a social revolution, but which I will call in the present context the expansion of reason, is only just beginning. But it is advancing at a staggering pace to keep abreast of the staggering technological advances of the last generation. It seems to me one of the major aspects of our twentieth-century revolution.

Some of our pessimists and sceptics will certainly call me to order if I fail at this point to notice the dangers and the ambiguous aspects of the role assigned to reason in the contemporary world. In an earlier lecture I pointed out that increasing individualization in the sense described did not imply any weakening of social pressures for conformity and uniformity. This is indeed one of the paradoxes of our complex modern society. Education, which is a necessary and powerful instrument in promoting the expansion of individual capacities and opportunities, and therefore of increasing individualization, is also a powerful instrument in the hands of interested groups for promoting social uniformity. Pleas frequently heard for more responsible broadcasting and television, or for a more responsible press, are directed in the first instance against certain negative phenomena which it is easy to condemn. But they quickly become pleas to use these powerful instruments of mass perusasion in order to inculcate desirable tastes and desirable opinions — the standard of

[1] *Vierteljahrshefte für Zeitgeschichte* (Munich), i (1953), 38.

desirability being found in the accepted tastes and opinions of the society. Such campaigns, in the hands of those who promote them, are conscious and rational processes designed to shape society, by shaping its individual members, in a desired direction. Other glaring examples of these dangers are provided by the commercial advertiser and the political propagandist. The two roles are, indeed, frequently doubled; openly in the United States, and rather more sheepishly in Great Britain, parties and candidates employ professional advertisers to put themselves across. The two procedures, even when formally distinct, are remarkably similar. Professional advertisers and the heads of the propaganda departments of great political parties are highly intelligent men who bring all the resources of reason to bear on their task. Reason, however, as in the other instances we have examined is employed not for mere exploration, but constructively, not statically, but dynamically. Professional advertisers and campaign managers are not primarily concerned with existing facts. They are interested in what the consumer or elector now believes or wants only in so far as this enters into the end-product, *i.e.* what the consumer or elector can by skilful handling be induced to believe or want. Moreover, their study of mass psychology has shown them that the most rapid way to secure acceptance of their views is through an appeal to the irrational element in the make-up of the customer and elector, so that the picture which confronts us is one in which an élite of professional industrialists or party leaders, through rational processes more highly developed than ever before, attains its ends by understanding and trading on the irrationalism of the masses. The appeal is not primarily to reason: it proceeds in the main by the method which Oscar Wilde called 'hitting below the intellect'. I have somewhat overdrawn the pricture lest I should be accused of underestimating the danger.[1] But it is broadly correct, and could easily be

[1] For a fuller discussion see the author's *The New Society* (1951), ch. 4 *passim.*

applied to other spheres. In every society, more or less coercive measures are applied by ruling groups to organize and control mass opinion. This method seems worse than some because it constitutes an abuse of reason.

In reply to this serious and well-founded indictment I have only two arguments. The first is the familiar one that every invention, every innovation, every new technique discovered in the course of history has had its negative as well as its positive sides. The cost has always to be borne by somebody. I do not know how long it was after the invention of printing before critics began to point out that it facilitated the spread of erroneous opinions. Today it is a commonplace to lament the death-roll on the roads caused by the advent of the motor-car ; and even some scientists deplore their own discovery of ways and means to release atomic energy because of the catastrophic uses to which it can be, and has been, put. Such objections have not availed in the past, and seem unlikely to avail in the future, to stay the advance of new discoveries and inventions. What we have learned of the techniques and potentialities of mass propaganda cannot be simply obliterated. It is no more possible to return to the small-scale individualist democracy of Lockeian or liberal theory, partially realized in Great Britain in the middle years of the nineteenth century, than it is possible to return to the horse and buggy or to early *laissez-faire* capitalism. But the true answer is that these evils also carry with them their own corrective. The remedy lies not in a cult of irrationalism or a renunciation of the extended role of reason in modern society, but in a growing consciousness from below as well as from above of the role which reason can play. This is not a utopian dream at a time when the increasing use of reason at all levels of society is being forced on us by our technological and scientific revolution. Like every other great advance in history, this advance has its costs and its losses, which have to be paid, and its dangers, which have to be faced. Yet, in spite of sceptics, and cynics, and prophets of disaster, especially among the intellectuals of countries whose former privileged position has been under-mined, I shall not be ashamed to treat it as a signal example of progress in the history. It is perhaps the most striking and revolutionary phenomenon of our time.

The second aspect of the progressive revolution through which we are passing is the changed shape of the world. The great period of the fifteenth and sixteenth centuries, in which the mediaeval world finally broke up in ruins and the founda-tions of the modern world were laid, was marked by the dis-covery of new continents and by the passing of the world centre of gravity from the shores of the Mediterranean to those of the Atlantic. Even the lesser upheaval of the French revolution had its geographical sequel in the calling in of the new world to redress the balance of the old. But the changes wrought by the twentieth-century revolution are far more sweeping than anything that has happened since the sixteenth century. After some 400 years the world centre of gravity has definitely shifted away from western Europe. Western Europe, together with the outlying parts of the English-speaking world, has become an appanage of the North Ameri-can continent, or, if you like, an agglomeration in which the United States serves both as power-house and as control-tower. Nor is this the only, or perhaps the most significant, change. It is by no means clear that the world centre of gravity now resides, or will continue for long to reside, in the English-speaking world with its western European annex. It appears to be the great land-mass of eastern Europe and Asia, with its extensions into Africa, which today calls the tune in world affairs. The 'unchanging east' is nowadays a singularly worn-out cliché.

Let us take a quick look at what has happened to Asia in the present century. The story begins with the Anglo-Japanese alliance of 1902 — the first admission of an Asiatic country to the charmed circle of European Great Powers. It may perhaps be regarded as a coincidence that Japan signalized her promotion by challenging and defeating Russia, and, in so doing, kindled the first spark which ignited the great twentieth-century revolution. The French revolutions of 1789 and 1848 had found their imitators in Europe. The first Russian revolution of 1905 awakened no echo in Europe, but found its imitators in Asia : in the next few years revolutions occurred in Persia, in Turkey and in China. The first World War was not precisely a world war, but a European civil war — assuming that such an entity as Europe existed — with world-wide consequences : these included the stimulation of industrial development in many Asian countries, of anti-foreign feeling in China and of Indian nationalism, and the birth of Arab nationalism. The Russian revolution of 1917 provided a further and decisive impulse. What was significant here was that its leaders looked persistently, but in vain, for imitators in Europe, and finally found them in Asia. It was Europe that had become 'unchanging', Asia that was on the move. I need not continue this familiar story down to the present time. The historian is hardly yet in a position to assess the scope and significance of the Asian and African revolution. But the spread of modern technological and industrial processes, and of the beginnings of education and political consciousness, to millions of the population of Asia and Africa, is changing the face of those continents ; and, while I cannot peer into the future, I do not know of any standard of judgment which would allow me to regard this as anything but a progressive development in the perspective of world history. The changed shape of the world resulting from these events has brought with it a relative decline in the weight, certainly of this country, perhaps of the English-speaking countries as a whole, in world affairs. But relative decline is not absolute decline ; and what disturbs and alarms me is not the march of progress in Asia and Africa, but the tendency of dominant groups in this country — and perhaps elsewhere — to turn a blind or uncomprehending eye on these developments, to adopt towards them an attitude oscillating between mistrustful disdain and affable condescension, and to sink back into a paralyzing nostalgia for the past.

What I have called the expansion of reason in our twentieth-century revolution has particular consequences for the historian ; for the expansion of reason means, in essence, the emergence into history of groups and classes, of peoples and continents that hitherto lay outside it. In my first lecture I suggested that the tendency of mediaeval historians to view mediaeval society through the spectacles of religion was due to the exclusive character of their sources. I should like to pursue this explanation a little further. It has, I think, correctly, though no doubt with some exaggeration, been said that the Christian church was 'the one rational institution of the Middle Ages'.[1] Being the one rational institution, it was the one historical institution ; it alone was subject to a rational course of development which could be comprehended by the historian. Secular society was moulded and organized by the church, and had no rational life of its own. The mass of people belonged, like pre-historic peoples, to nature rather than to history. Modern history begins when more and more people emerge into social and political consciousness, become aware of their respective groups as historical entities having a past and a future, and enter fully into history. It is only within the last 200 years at most, even in a few advanced countries, that social, political and historical consciousness have begun to spread to anything like a majority of the population. It is only today that it has become possible for the first time even to imagine a whole world consisting of peoples who have in the fullest sense entered into history and become the concern, no longer of the colonial administrator or of the anthropologist, but of the historian.

This is a revolution in our conception of history. In the eighteenth century history was still a history of élites. In the

[1] A. von Martin, *The Sociology of the Renaissance* (Engl. transl., 1945), p. 18.

nineteenth century British historians began, haltingly and spasmodically, to advance towards a view of history as the history of the whole national community. J. R. Green, a rather pedestrian historian, won fame by writing the first *History of the English People*. In the twentieth century every historian pays lip-service to this view; and, though performance lags behind profession, I shall not dwell on these shortcomings, since I am much more concerned with our failure as historians to take account of the widening horizon of history outside this country and outside western Europe. Acton in his report of 1896 spoke of universal history as 'that which is distinct from the combined history of all countries'. He continued:

> It moves in a succession to which the nations are subsidiary. Their story will be told, not for their own sake, but in reference and subordination to a higher series, according to the time and degree in which they contribute to the common fortunes of mankind.[1]

It went without saying for Acton that universal history, as he conceived it, was the concern of any serious historian. What are we at present doing to facilitate the approach to universal history in this sense?

I did not intend in these lectures to touch on the study of history in this university: but it provides me with such striking examples of what I am trying to say that it would be cowardly of me to avoid grasping the nettle. In the past forty years we have made a substantial place in our curriculum for the history of the United States. This is an important advance. But it has carried with it a certain risk of reinforcing the parochialism of English history, which already weighs like a dead hand on our curriculum, with a more insidious and equally dangerous parochialism of the English-speaking world. The history of the English-speaking world in the last

[1] *Cambridge Modern History: Its Origin, Authorship and Production* (1907), p. 14.

400 years has beyond question been a great period of history. But to treat it as the centre-piece of universal history, and everything else as peripheral to it, is an unhappy distortion of perspective. It is the duty of a university to correct such popular distortions. The school of modern history in this university seems to me to fall short in the discharge of this duty. It is surely wrong that a candidate should be allowed to sit for an honours degree in history in a major university without an adequate knowledge of any modern language other than English; let us take warning by what happened in Oxford to the ancient and respected discipline of philosophy when its practitioners came to the conclusion that they could get on very nicely with plain everyday English. It is surely wrong that no facilities should be offered to the candidate to study the modern history of any continental European country above the text-book level. A candidate possessing some knowledge of the affairs of Asia, Africa or Latin America has at present a very limited opportunity of displaying it in a paper called with magnificent nineteenth-century *panache* 'The Expansion of Europe'. The title unfortunately fits the contents: the candidate is not invited to know anything even of countries with an important and well-documented history like China or Persia except what happened when the Europeans attempted to take them over. Lectures are, I am told, delivered in this university on the history of Russia and Persia and China — but not by members of the faculty of history. The conviction expressed by the professor of Chinese in his inaugural lecture five years ago that 'China cannot be regarded as outside the mainstream of human history'[1] has fallen on deaf ears among Cambridge historians. What may well be regarded in the future as the greatest historical work produced in Cambridge during the past decade has been written entirely outside the history department, and without any assistance from it: I refer to Dr. Needham's *Science and Civilization in*

[1] E. G. Pulleyblank, *Chinese History and World History* (1955), p. 36.

*China.* This is a sobering thought. I should not have exposed these domestic sores to the public gaze but for the fact that I believe them to be typical of most other British universities and of British intellectuals in general in the middle years of the twentieth century. That stale old quip about Victorian insularity, 'Storms in the Channel — the Continent Isolated', has an uncomfortably topical ring today. Once more storms are raging in the world beyond ; and, while we in the English-speaking countries huddle together and tell ourselves in plain everyday English that other countries and other continents are isolated by their extraordinary behaviour from the boons and blessings of our civilization, it sometimes looks as if we, by our inability or unwillingness to understand, were isolating ourselves from what is really going on in the world.

In the opening sentences of my first lecture I drew attention to the sharp difference of outlook which separates the middle years of the twentieth century from the last years of the nineteenth. I should like in conclusion to develop this contrast ; and, if in this context I use the words 'liberal' and 'conservative', it will be readily understood that I am not using them in their sense as labels for British political parties. When Acton spoke of progress, he did not think in terms of the popular British concept of 'gradualism'. 'The Revolution, or as we say Liberalism', is a striking phrase from a letter of 1887. 'The method of modern progress', he said in a lecture on modern history ten years later, 'was revolution' ; and in another lecture he spoke of 'the advent of general ideas which we call revolution'. This is explained in one of his unpublished manuscript notes : 'The Whig governed by compromise : the Liberal begins the reign of ideas'.[1] Acton believed

[1] For these passages see Acton, *Selections from Correspondence* (1917), p. 278 ; *Lectures on Modern History* (1906), pp. 4, 32 ; Add MSS. 4949 (in Cambridge University Library). In the letter of 1887 quoted above Acton marks the change from the 'old' to the 'new' Whigs (*i.e.* the Liberals) as 'the discovery of conscience' : 'conscience' here is evidently

that 'the reign of ideas' meant liberalism, and that liberalism meant revolution. In Acton's lifetime, liberalism had not yet spent its force as a dynamic of social change. In our day, what survives of liberalism has everywhere become a conservative factor in society. It would be meaningless today to preach a return to Acton. But the historian is concerned, first to establish where Acton stood, secondly to contrast his position with that of contemporary thinkers, and thirdly to enquire what elements in his position may be still valid today. The generation of Acton suffered, no doubt, from overweening self-confidence and optimism, and did not sufficiently realize the precarious nature of the structure on which its faith rested. But it possessed two things of both of which we are badly in need today : a sense of change as a progressive factor in history, and belief in reason as our guide for the understanding of its complexities.

Let us now listen to some voices of the 1950s. I quoted in an earlier lecture Sir Lewis Namier's expression of satisfaction that, while 'practical solutions' were sought for 'concrete problems', 'programmes and ideals are forgotten by both parties', and his description of this as a symptom of 'national maturity'.[1] I am not fond of these analogies between the life-span of individuals and that of nations ; and, if such an analogy is invoked, it tempts one to ask what follows when we have passed the stage of 'maturity'. But what interests me is the sharp contrast drawn between the practical and the concrete, which are praised, and 'programmes and ideals', which are condemned. This exaltation of practical action over idealistic theorizing is, of course, the hall-mark of

associated with the development of 'consciousness' (see p. 130 above), and corresponds to 'the reign of ideas'. Stubbs also divided modern history into two periods separated by the French revolution : 'the first a history of powers, forces and dynasties ; the second, a history in which ideas take the place of both rights and forms' (W. Stubbs, *Seventeen Lectures on the Study of Mediaeval and Modern History* (3rd ed., 1900), p. 239).

[1] See p. 33 above.

conservatism. In Namier's thought it represents the voice of the eighteenth century, of the England at the accession of George III, protesting against the impending onset of Acton's revolution and reign of ideas. But the same familiar expression of out-and-out conservatism in the form of out-and-out empiricism is highly popular in our day. It may be found in its most popular form in Professor Trevor-Roper's remark that, 'when radicals scream that victory is indubitably theirs, sensible conservatives knock them on the nose'.[1] Professor Oakeshott offers us a more sophisticated version of this fashionable empiricism : in our political concerns, he tells us, we 'sail a boundless and bottomless sea', where there is 'neither starting-point nor appointed destination', and where our sole aim can be 'to keep afloat on an even keel'.[2] I need not pursue the catalogue of recent writers who have denounced political 'utopianism' and 'messianism' ; these have become the current terms of opprobrium for far-reaching radical ideas on the future of society. Nor shall I attempt to discuss recent trends in the United States, where historians and political theorists have had less inhibitions than their colleagues in this country in openly proclaiming their allegiance to conservatism. I will quote only a remark by one of the most distinguished and most moderate of American conservative historians, Professor Samuel Morison of Harvard, who in his presidential address to the American Historical Association in December 1950 thought that the time had come for a reaction against what he called 'the Jefferson-Jackson-F. D. Roosevelt line' and pleaded for a history of the United States 'written from a sanely conservative point of view'.[3]

But it is Professor Popper who, at any rate in Great Britain, has once more expressed this cautious conservative outlook in its clearest and most uncompromising form.

---

[1] *Encounter*, vii, No. 6, June 1957, p. 17.
[2] M. Oakeshott, *Political Education* (1951), p. 22.
[3] *American Historical Review*, No. lvi, No. 2 (January 1951), pp. 272-273.

Echoing Namier's rejection of 'programmes and ideals', he attacks policies which allegedly aim at 're-modelling the "whole of society" in accordance with a definite plan', commends what he calls 'piecemeal social engineering', and does not apparently shrink from the imputation of 'piecemeal tinkering' and 'muddling through'.[1]  On one point, indeed, I should pay tribute to Professor Popper.  He remains a stout defender of reason, and will have no truck with past or present excursions into irrationalism.  But, if we look into his prescription of 'piecemeal social engineering', we shall see how limited is the role which he assigns to reason.  Though his definition of 'piecemeal engineering' is not very precise, we are specifically told that criticism of 'ends' is excluded ; and the cautious examples which he gives of its legitimate activities — 'constitutional reform' and 'a tendency towards a greater equalization of incomes' — show plainly that it is intended to operate within the assumptions of our existing society.[2]  The status of reason in Professor Popper's scheme of things is, in fact, rather like that of a British civil servant, qualified to administer the policies of the government in power and even to suggest practical improvements to make them work better, but not to question their fundamental presuppositions or ultimate purposes.  This is useful work : I, too, have been a civil servant in my day.  But this subordination of reason to the assumptions of the existing order seems to me in the long run wholly unacceptable.  This is not how Acton thought of reason when he propounded his equation, revolution = liberalism = the reign of ideas.  Progress in human affairs, whether in science or in history or in society, has come mainly through the bold readiness of human beings not to confine themselves to seeking piecemeal improvements in the way things are done, but to present fundamental challenges in the name of reason to the current way of doing things and to the avowed or hidden assumptions on which it rests.  I

[1] K. Popper, *The Poverty of Historicism* (1957), pp. 67, 74.
[2] *Ibid.* pp. 64, 68.

look forward to a time when the historians and sociologists and political thinkers of the English-speaking world will regain their courage for that task.

It is, however, not the waning of faith in reason among the intellectuals and the political thinkers of the English-speaking world which perturbs me most, but the loss of the pervading sense of a world in perpetual motion. This seems at first sight paradoxical; for rarely has so much superficial talk been heard of changes going on around us. But the significant thing is that change is no longer thought of as achievement, as opportunity, as progress, but as an object of fear. When our political and economic pundits prescribe, they have nothing to offer us but the warning to mistrust radical and far-reaching ideas, to shun anything that savours of revolution, and to advance — if advance we must — as slowly and cautiously as we can. At a moment when the world is changing its shape more rapidly and more radically than at any time in the last 400 years, this seems to me a singular blindness, which gives ground for apprehension, not that the world-wide movement will be stayed, but that this country — and perhaps other English-speaking countries — may lag behind the general advance, and relapse helplessly and uncomplainingly into some nostalgic backwater. For myself I remain an optimist; and when Sir Lewis Namier warns me to eschew programmes and ideals, and Professor Oakeshott tells me that we are going nowhere in particular and that all that matters is to see that nobody rocks the boat, and Professor Popper wants to keep that dear old T-model on the road by dint of a little piecemeal engineering, and Professor Trevor-Roper knocks screaming radicals on the nose, and Professor Morison pleads for history written in a sane conservative spirit, I shall look out on a world in tumult and a world in travail, and shall answer in the well-worn words of a great scientist: 'And yet — it moves'.

# Index